Joseph Meloche, MLIS

Introductory CD ROM Searching: The Key to Effective Ondisc Searching

Prepublication REVIEWS, COMMENTARIES, EVALUATIONS . . .

"THIS BOOK FILLS A GAP IN THE LITERATURE OF INFORMATION RETRIEVAL. It is also useful in its accessible approach to the use of this technology; thus this publication can be used by a wide range of people, starting with students in upper high schools to students in colleges and universities, even library professionals who are somewhat new to this technology. I would highly recommend it for libraries of these institutions."

Gulten S. Wagner, PhD
School of Information and Library Studies, Curtin University of Technology, Western Australia

More pre-publication
REVIEWS, COMMENTARIES, EVALUATIONS . . .

"AN IDEAL BEGINNER'S GUIDE TO CD ROM SEARCHING WITHOUT TEARS. It will be equally useful for students in library schools, for reference librarians wishing to update their skills, and for the end-user in libraries of all types.

Part I introduces the novice to the essential concepts, assuming no prior knowledge, and explains the terminology carefully, with many useful examples.

Part II covers the specific searching procedures of different databases presently available on the market. Techniques for successful searching on each one are demonstrated with examples from actual searches that the student can replicate."

A VERY PRACTICAL AND WELL-PACED GUIDE THAT WILL BE INVALUABLE FOR STUDENTS, LIBRARIANS, AND ALL CD ROM USERS."

Neil A. Radford, PhD
University Librarian,
The University of Sydney

"THE BOOK IS AN EXCELLENT GUIDE FOR THE NOVICE CD ROM USER. It gives basic instructions for searching techniques and for the utilization of Ondisc information. It also serves as a reference source to the user of various CD ROM products.

The carefully selected search examples, as well as the Summary and Review Questions following the main chapters are witness to the author's pedagogical talents. He should also be credited for the pleasant style and easy-going language in which he presents the reasons for and details of Ondisc searching.

The Glossary and a Summary list of the major CD ROMS grouped by subject area add further value to the book, which is really a 'friendly tutor' for beginners of Ondisc searching."

Irene Wormell, Professor
The Royal School of Librarianship,
Copenhagen, Denmark

The Haworth Press, Inc.

NOTES FOR PROFESSIONAL LIBRARIANS AND LIBRARY USERS

This is an original book title published by The Haworth Press, Inc. Unless otherwise noted in specific chapters with attribution, materials in this book have not been previously published elsewhere in any format or language.

CONSERVATION AND PRESERVATION NOTES

All books published by The Haworth Press, Inc. are printed on certified ph neutral, acid free book grade paper. This conforms to recommendations ensuring a book's long life without deterioration.

Introductory CD ROM Searching
The Key to Effective Ondisc Searching

HAWORTH Library and Information Science
Peter Gellatly, Editor in Chief

New, Recent, and Forthcoming Titles:

The In-House Option: Professional Issues of Library Automation by T. D. Webb

British University Libraries by Toby Burrows

Women Online: Perspectives on Women's Studies in Online Databases edited by Steven D. Atkinson and Judith Hudson

Buyers and Borrowers: The Application of Consumer Theory to the Study of Library Use by Charles D. Emery

Broadway's Prize-Winning Musicals: An Annotated Guide for Libraries and Audio Collectors by Leo N. Miletich

Introductory CD ROM Searching: The Key to Effective Ondisc Searching by Joseph Meloche

Academic Libraries in Greece: The Present Situation and Future Prospects edited by Dean H. Keller

Libraries and the Future: Essays on the Library in the Twenty-First Century by F. W. Lancaster

Dictionary of Bibliometrics by Virgil Diodato

Guide to Publishing Opportunities for Librarians by Carol Schroeder and Gloria Roberson

Introductory CD ROM Searching
The Key to Effective Ondisc Searching

Joseph Meloche, MLIS

The Haworth Press
New York • London • Norwood (Australia)

© 1994 by The Haworth Press, Inc. All rights reserved. No part of this work may be reproduced or utilized in any form or by any means, electronic or mechanical, including photocopying, microfilm and recording, or by any information storage and retrieval system, without permission in writing from the publisher. Printed in the United States of America.

The Haworth Press, Inc., 10 Alice Street, Binghamton, NY 13904-1580

Library of Congress Cataloging-in-Publication Data

Meloche, Joseph.
    Introductory CD ROM searching : the key to effective Ondisc searching / Joseph Meloche.
      p.   cm.
    Includes bibliographical references and index.
    ISBN 1-56024-412-7 (acid free paper).
    1. Online bibliographic searching–United States. 2. CD-ROM–United States. I. Title.
Z699.35.O55M44   1993
025.3'132–dc20
                                                                       92-44616
                                                                               CIP

CONTENTS

Preface	ix
Introduction	1

PART I: ESSENTIALS OF ONDISC SEARCHING

Chapter 1: Ondisc Searching	5
What Is Ondisc Searching?	5
Information Available	6
Basic Components of Ondisc Searching	7
Databases	7
Equipment	8
Locating the Items	8
Summary	10
Review Questions	11
Chapter 2: Basic Searching Strategies	13
Three Basic Steps in the Ondisc Search	13
Boolean Logic	16
Searching Techniques	20
Summary	26
Review Questions	27
Chapter 3: Record Structures	29
Records	29
Field-Specific Searching	31
Record Structures	31
Field Keys	32
Summary	36
Review Questions	37

Chapter 4: The Microcomputer   39

Types of Microcomputers   39
Formatting   40
The Keyboard   41
The Results   42
Downloading   42
Uploading   43
Macintosh Computers   43
Summary   44
Review Questions   44

PART II: PRODUCT-SPECIFIC SEARCHING

Chapter 5: DIALOG Ondisc Searching   47

Sources of Information   47
Truncation   59
Downloading and Printing in the Command Search Mode   61

Chapter 6: SilverPlatter Ondisc Searching   63

Sources of Information   63
PsycLIT Database   64
Searching on SilverPlatter-PsycLIT   66
Special Features   78
Printing Records   79
Downloading Records   79

Chapter 7: WILSONDISC Searching   81

Sources of Information   81
Searching on WILSONDISC   85
Downloading and Printing   92

Chapter 8: UMI Searching   95

Sources of Information   95
Searching ABI/INFORM Ondisc   98
Downloading   108

Chapter 9: Compact Cambridge Searching   111

    Sources of Information   111
    Health Database   112
    Searching the Health Database   112
    Downloading   129

Chapter 10: AUSTROM Searching   131

    Sources of Information   131
    Searching AUSTROM–Overview   133
    Searching APAIS on AUSTROM   136
    Downloading Records   150
    Printing Records   151

Chapter 11: Grolier Encyclopedia   153

    The New Grolier Electronic Encyclopedia   153
    Full-Text Searching   153
    Picture Retrieval   155
    Advanced Searching Techniques   155
    Special Features   162

Chapter 12: ISI® Citation Indexes–Social Sciences Citation Index® and Science Citation Index®   165

    Sources of Information   165
    Searching the Social Sciences Citation Index®   166
    Record Structure   168
    Using the Citation Dictionaries   169
    Boolean Searching   173
    Advanced Features   177
    Printing and Downloading Documents   178
    Summary   180

Appendix A: A Summary List of the Major CD ROMs by Subject Area   181

Appendix B: Glossary   191

Index   197

ABOUT THE AUTHOR

Joseph A. Meloche, MLIS, PhD (cand.), is a Lecturer working in the area of information retrieval and new technology with the University of Technology, Sydney. In his previous position he was a Senior Subject Librarian and the CD ROM coordinator at the University of Sydney's Fisher Library, the largest academic library in Australia. In 1991, he worked as a lecturer at Curtin University of Technology, where he discovered a dearth of information on CD ROM and began his work on this text. His professional experience also includes working as the Systems librarian with Sydney College of Advanced Education, where he introduced CD ROM technology to the College Library. He has written and presented papers for national and international conferences on the topic of information retrieval and CD ROM technology and is active as a consultant/researcher in this area. He is currently undertaking a doctorate with the University of New South Wales, researching the impact of optical disc technology in Australian academic institutions.

Preface

This book was written for the novice CD ROM user. In my experience as a lecturer in Library and Information Sciences, I have taught both undergraduates and postgraduates the principles of on-disc searching. I discovered that no works were available to show students the basics of searching for information ondisc. This book is written to fill this gap and to provide all novice CD ROM users with the basics of ondisc searching.

The writing of this book began when I was working as a lecturer with Curtin University's School of Information and Library Studies. Since that time I have returned to my substantive position as a Senior Subject Librarian with the University of Sydney Library, where I am the Coordinator of CD ROM Services in the Main Reference Library. I have enjoyed support for this project from both institutions.

The writing of this book required that I conduct a number of searches as examples. The equipment that I used for these searches included a Pioneer CD ROM changer. This product has the advantage of allowing up to six CD ROMs to be loaded at a time. This equipment and the titles used as examples were supplied by Caroline Beatty, Product Manager with CD ROM and Associates of Melbourne, Victoria. The production of this work would not have been feasible without her support.

There are too many people who have given me both advice and support to list them all here, but I thank them. I will, however, mention those who contributed directly to this work. First, I would like to thank my wife, Yumiko, who has shown tremendous patience and has always given me encouragement during the course of writing this book. I would also like to thank Margaret Sheppard who, as a friend and mentor, has–in this and many ventures–given me assistance and insight into my work. Finally I wish to thank my former student and current research assistant, Bonnie Siu, who has given her time to this work. The chart in Figure 7 and Appendix A are just two examples of her many contributions. Her continuing assistance and thoughtful advice have benefited this work.

It is my hope that students will find this a useful first guide and that they will become regular users of ondisc databases.

Joseph Meloche
Sydney, Australia

Introduction

Introductory CD ROM Searching is a beginners' guide to searching databases on CD ROM. The expression ondisc searching is used in this book to refer to searching for information using CD ROM databases.

CD ROM is the acronym for Compact Disc Read Only Memory. For now it will suffice to define CD ROMs as a storage and retrieval medium. CD ROMs have been available to the public since 1985, but it is only in the 1990s that their impact has been felt strongly in libraries. A single CD ROM disc contains an amount of information equivalent to about 220,000 pages of text, or 1,500 floppy discs, or 6 volumes of an encyclopedia. CD ROM technology has brought database access to the level of the microcomputer. This is significant in two ways. First, CD ROMs provide you with access to huge commercial databases without either time or telecommunication charges. Second, it has given libraries local control over this resource, which can mean unrestricted access up to 24 hours a day. It is hardly surprising that CD ROMs are immensely popular and in high demand.

It is not the purpose of this book to explain the technical aspects of CD ROM technology or the different means by which a CD ROM system may be established. Its aim is to give *you* basic instruction in the *searching techniques* that you will need to fully utilize the benefits of ondisc information. Thus, the purpose of the book is to show the basic searching strategies and logic that are common to all ondisc searching.

In Part I you will be introduced to the essentials of ondisc searching. The first four chapters explain the reasons for ondisc searching and introduce record structures, databases, searching techniques, Boolean logic, and microcomputers. Part I is essential reading for the new ondisc searcher.

In the second part of this book, Part II, the major ondisc software is introduced along with the specific searching protocols that are likely to be encountered. This section allows you to see searching procedures used in specific instances. Part II will serve as a reference source as you begin to use a variety of ondisc products.

Appendix A provides a subject listing of major ondisc databases. The Glossary (Appendix B) gives definitions of terms introduced in this work.

PART I:
ESSENTIALS OF ONDISC SEARCHING

Chapter 1

Ondisc Searching

WHAT IS ONDISC SEARCHING?

In this chapter you will be introduced to ondisc searching and given the opportunity to learn the basic components of ondisc searching. The searches you conduct will illustrate the wealth of material available ondisc and how that material can be obtained from ondisc searching after only a small investment of your time.

You will find that searching ondisc is an effective, fun, and current means of accessing information. The value of ondisc searching is that it can provide *every* library user with access to major databases and information sources. In many cases, it is a direct replacement for, or alternative to, a printed product. You will find numerous advantages to having material available ondisc. These advantages relate to methods of information retrieval that were previously the domain of the reference librarian or professional researcher. Prior to the advent of CD ROMs, online searching was the only alternative to using printed sources. Online searching, while an extremely effective means of information retrieval, was one that was rarely made available to the public, nor was it ever intended to be. CD ROMs, however, are available to patrons of university and college libraries, school libraries, and, increasingly, public libraries.

Ondisc searching involves searching a database of machine-readable information that is stored in a digital format on a CD ROM disc. Searching ondisc is effective because it allows you to retrieve information by using combinations of search terms. Ondisc searching, the searching of information using Boolean logic, is what this book will introduce. Boolean logic is the basis of all ondisc and online searching. Boolean logic is based on the use of three logical operators: the **AND, OR,** and **NOT** operators. It is now possible to search huge databases of information and obtain precise results by using the Boolean operators. It will take practice before you begin to use the operators effectively, and it is extremely important that you learn to control their use. You will find that it can be as important to establish what has *not* been written or indexed as it is to uncover what *has* been written.

Ondisc searching will allow you to determine definitively what is included within a database. This is important since material is increasingly written and recorded only in machine-readable form and the information must be searched in a thorough manner. It is of equal importance that you acquaint yourself with the range of material covered by the databases that you search. It is your responsibility to select and search appropriate databases and to know the extent of the subject coverage of a database. The information provided in Appendix A gives you an overview of the subject coverage of a variety of databases.

INFORMATION AVAILABLE

The databases that you will search ondisc were, in most cases, created prior to the advent of ondisc searching. The machine-readable databases that you can now search ondisc were previously made available only for online searchers or as inhouse databases for government or private industry. There is, therefore, a wealth of material available ondisc despite its short history. Almost every subject area or discipline you can think of is now available ondisc. For example, just one product, AUSTROM, has 13 Australian social science and educational databases on a single disc. AUSTROM's sources of information include journal articles, reports, conference papers, theses, newspapers, books, and reviews of books. The subject areas for AUSTROM alone include the social sciences, humanities, education, sport, architecture, leisure, recreation and criminology. Of course, there are numerous international products that cover every possible area of interest. Business information, for example, is available through ABI/INFORM, a service that indexes over 800 business periodicals and offers the full text of the journals ondisc. The amount of material available ondisc and the range of computer facilities that make ondisc searching viable are both growing rapidly.

BASIC COMPONENTS OF ONDISC SEARCHING

The ondisc search begins with the user, *you*, and your need for information. The next step is for you to access material that has been written on the subject that you are researching. Ondisc searching is the process that allows you to search subject terms or keywords in databases of *records* that will provide you with citations and abstracts of published material related to your query. The *citations* will provide you with the source of the original publication and the *abstract* will give you a precis or outline of what is contained in the original publication. The *descriptors* and *identifiers* attached to the record will allow you to gain subject access to the record. Because the abstracts are searchable, they have the additional advantage of providing increased subject access to the record. The outcome of the successful search will be a number of citations that lead you to original publications of material related to your query.

DATABASES

Databases are the source of information that your search will query. A database is a collection of related information. The databases referred to within this text will, of course, be mounted on CD ROM discs. The database will typically be bibliographic and refer to a specific subject area or discipline; however, many other types of databases are available. These include dictionaries, encyclopedias, full text sources, and graphic databases.

Databases can be divided into the following major categories:

    a. Bibliographic databases (indexes, abstracts, etc.)
    b. Source or nonbibliographic material (dictionaries, encyclopedias, collections of facts, etc.)

 c. Full text databases
 d. Statistical databases
 e. Graphic databases

EQUIPMENT

 Before you actually start searching you will need to consider the type of equipment that you are likely to encounter. The first item common to all ondisc searching is the disc itself. A CD ROM disc is physically similar to the CD that you would use in a home stereo. Like the home stereo disc which requires a CD player, the CD ROM disc requires a CD ROM player or a CD ROM reader, as it is referred to in this text. The CD ROM reader will always be one component of a CD ROM workstation. There are several possible configurations for the CD ROM workstation, a few common CD ROM workstation configurations are listed below.

 The most basic CD ROM workstation (see Figure 1) will include a microcomputer and a single CD ROM reader in which the CD ROM disc would need to be inserted each time it is used. The better system would consist of a network of microcomputers with a number of CD ROM products mounted remotely and selected via a menu. In the case of a networked system, it is unlikely that you would see either the CD ROM reader or the CD ROM disc. What you would encounter is the microcomputer. The microcomputer will be looked at in depth in Chapter 4. A knowledge of microcomputers, while not essential, is extremely useful if you wish to take full advantage of the technology. In the later sections you will be shown the procedures for downloading information to a floppy disc. Downloading, like searching, is a product-specific function and thus will be covered in depth when you look at the different vendors. You will also be shown how to upload the saved information to your word-processing software.

LOCATING THE ITEMS

 Once you have successfully retrieved records from your search request, and after you have decided which articles you wish to

FIGURE 1. CD ROM Workstation

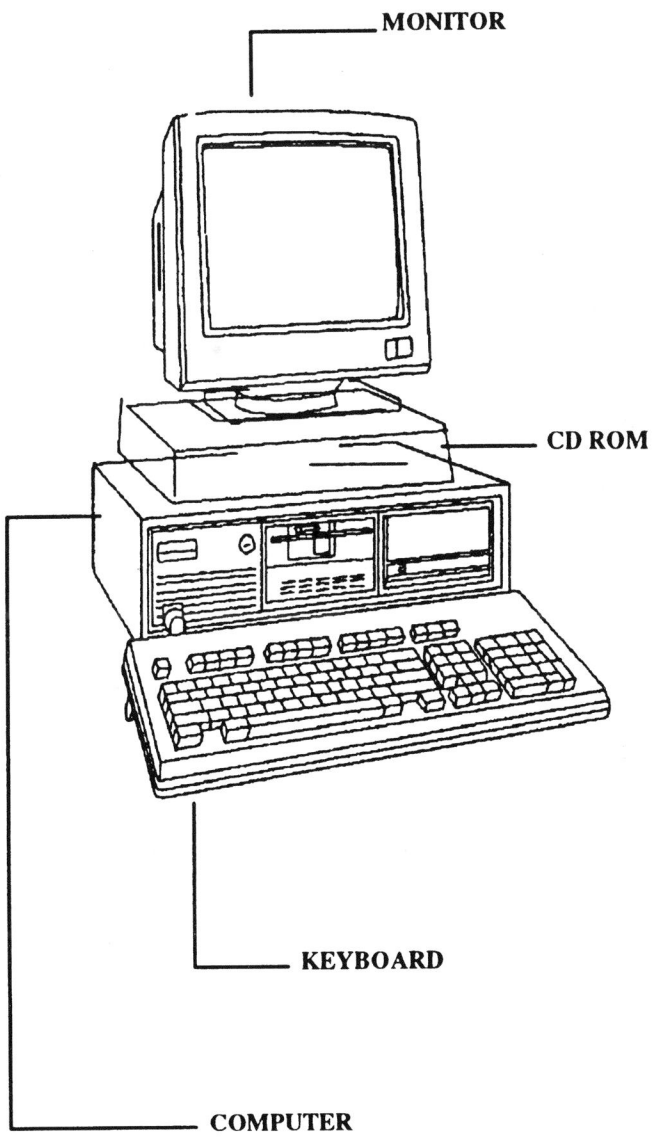

locate, you will need to use your library's catalog. The information that you need to take to the OPAC (Online Public Access Catalogue) or card catalog is the title of the journal or book that you need to locate. Entering the title into the OPAC or looking it up in the card catalog will give a call number or shelf number that will allow you to locate the material in the library. If the journal or book is not held by the library, ask one of the librarians on duty for advice on obtaining it.

SUMMARY

In this chapter you have been introduced to the concept of ondisc searching and the vast sources of information that are available via CD ROM technology. You should now be aware of the following:

a. The range of information available ondisc includes all subject areas or disciplines, and the amount of information available is increasing rapidly.
b. Information is arranged into databases, and databases are mounted on CD ROM discs.
c. The form of the information that is retrieved can vary. It will range from citations with abstracts, to full text sources, to nontext sources (i.e., graphic and statistical sources).
d. The amount or volume of the information available is only one of the advantages of ondisc searching. The real power of ondisc searching comes from the ability to retrieve information by using combinations of search terms.

This chapter also includes information about the equipment that you are likely to encounter. The equipment will typically include the following:

– the CD ROM reader or player
– the microcomputer (i.e., monitor, computer unit, keyboard, disc drives)
– the printer

REVIEW QUESTIONS

1. CD ROM is the acronym for _____ _____ _____ _____ _____.
2. In what format is information stored on a CD ROM?
3. Give three examples of how much information a single CD ROM disc can hold.
4. What is the minimum equipment you need for a single CD ROM workstation?
5. Name the main advantages of ondisc searching.

Chapter 2
Basic Searching Strategies

In this chapter you will be shown how to develop search strategies and how to make effective use of the searching logic that is used for all ondisc searching: Boolean logic. Boolean logic will be explained and examples of searching using the Boolean operators will be shown. Other searching techniques that this chapter introduces include the use of truncation operators, controlled vocabulary, and field specific searching.

THREE BASIC STEPS IN THE ONDISC SEARCH

To begin, consider the three basic steps used when ondisc searching.

The first step is the creation of the search question. This is an important step as it allows you to clarify your information need.

The second step is the identification of keywords from your search question. In this step you are also given the opportunity to reexamine your search question and expand upon it, if necessary.

The third step is the combination of the keywords or key concepts with the use of Boolean operators in a search query for use in an appropriate ondisc database.

You will find the above description an extreme simplification of a complex process. The process will work, however, if you keep the steps in mind and work through each step before moving on to the next step.

Step One: The Creation of the Search Question

This is perhaps the most interesting step as the ultimate success of your search may depend on the work you do at this stage. There are several techniques that will help you develop an appropriate search question.

Start by writing out, in rough form, the basic question that you want information about. For example, if your topic is *the effect of running on both health and fitness,* you might write the following:

> I would like to know if running helps to keep me fit and does running have any effect on my health? Does running impair my health in any way?

Step Two: The Identification of Keywords or Key Concepts

At the second step you start to refine your search statement by identifying *Keywords* or *Key Concepts* from the basic question. The keywords from the above query include Running, Fitness, and Health.

For this example you will begin with a simple but effective searching style. To start, break down the request into single queries.

Search A:

In this search you are seeking information about the effect of running on both health and fitness and AUSPORT is an appropriate database for this purpose.

You begin by identifying the key concepts in the above search request. The three key concepts are: *running, health,* and *fitness.* Once you have identified the key terms or concepts, you can prepare to begin your search. In the example below you will see how each term may be searched for separately. In the following illustration the **FIND** prompt is provided by the program.

FIND running

Set 1 = 150

FIND health

Set 2 = 350

FIND fitness

Set 3 = 25

In the above example the number following the set number (i.e., Set 1 = 150) is the number of records that contain the search term *running*.

The reason for searching in the above manner–for each term individually–is based on the flexibility that it gives you. For you may now choose to combine any or all of the above sets or even introduce new keywords. You can also manipulate the way that you combine the sets.

Step Three: The Combination
of Keywords or Key Concepts

The third step requires you to consider how you intend to link the keywords or key concepts that you have identified. To do this you will need to consider if the terms you identify represent similar or distinct concepts and whether you want to exclude specific terms or concepts from your search.

This step begins by giving thought to the extent or range of information that you wish to obtain. For example, do you wish to have every piece of material available on the subject or would you like to be more selective? Ask yourself the following types of questions.

   a. Do I want all the material written on the subject or only what was written recently, say in the last five years?
   b. Do I want material from all over the world or am I primarily interested in North American, European, or Australian material?
   c. Do I want information in all languages or am I only interested in English-language material?

Initially it would be useful to actually write out these questions and work through the steps one by one. In time, you will be able to work through the steps mentally as you develop your search question.

The actual search should not begin until you have answered the above questions. At this point, when you have finished the analysis of your search question, you will also need to consider the ondisc source that you wish to search. Your choice will depend on the way you answer the above questions.

To continue, assume that you made the following choices:

 a. recent material (i.e., for the previous five years)
 b. material from the political region of Australia
 c. English-language material

Before proceeding, it is necessary at this stage to look at Boolean operators in detail, to see how they may be used for combining keywords or key concepts to gain control over the search.

BOOLEAN LOGIC

The searching logic that is common to all ondisc searching is *Boolean logic*. It is Boolean logic that allows you to make use of combinations of sets and keywords. Boolean logic is the fundamental basis for all ondisc searching. It allows you to control your search through the use of three primary operators: the **AND**, the **OR**, and the **NOT** operators. Boolean logic can be illustrated with the use of Venn diagrams. Consider the following examples.

The first and most commonly used operator is the **AND** operator, which is used to associate two terms. (See Figure 2.) The use of the **AND** operator will narrow the search to retrieve only those records that contain *both* of the terms sought. Thus, in Figure 2 only the shaded area will be retrieved. This is because only this section contains both of the terms requested. For example, the request for **Fishing AND Trout** will retrieve only those records that contain both of the terms.

The second Boolean operator that will be examined is the **OR** operator. (See Figure 3.) The use of the **OR** operator will broaden the search to include all records that contain either term, or both of the terms. Thus, as shown in Figure 3, every section of both circles is retrieved. However, note that the circles still overlap; the reason for the overlap is that when the same record is retrieved by both of the terms searched, it is in fact only retrieved once. For example, a request for **Trout OR Perch** will retrieve all the records that con-

FIGURE 2. Fishing **AND** Trout

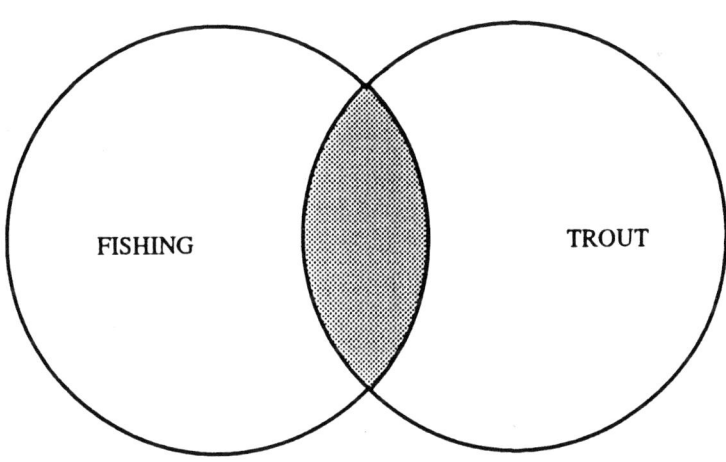

FIGURE 3. Trout **OR** Perch

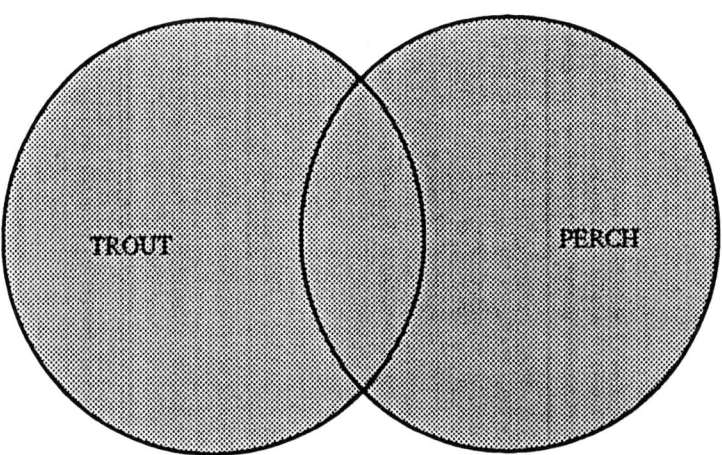

tain either of the terms as well as the records that contain *both* of the terms.

The third–and perhaps least used–operator is the **NOT** operator, which is used to dissociate two terms. (See Figure 4.) The use of the **NOT** operator will narrow the search by excluding all records that contain the term that you do not want to search. In Figure 4 the unshaded area represents those records that are excluded from the result set. Thus every occurrence of the term *Trout* is identified, and those records containing the excluded term are not included in your result set. For example, in the above case the request for **Fish NOT Trout** will retrieve only those records that contain the term *Fish* and do not contain the term *Trout*. **NOT** is a very powerful operator and needs to be used advisedly.

The real power of Boolean searching is realized when combinations of operators are used. A classic example is to combine one term using the **AND** operator with two other terms by placing an **OR** operator between them, as seen in Figure 5.

In Figure 5, *Running* is represented by Circle A, *Health* by Circle B, and *Fitness* by Circle C. Thus the shaded area where Circle A

FIGURE 4. Fish **NOT** Trout

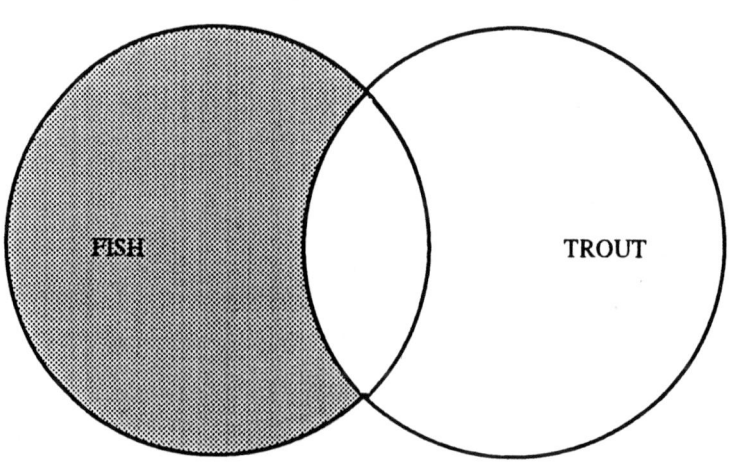

FIGURE 5. Running **AND** (Health **OR** Fitness)

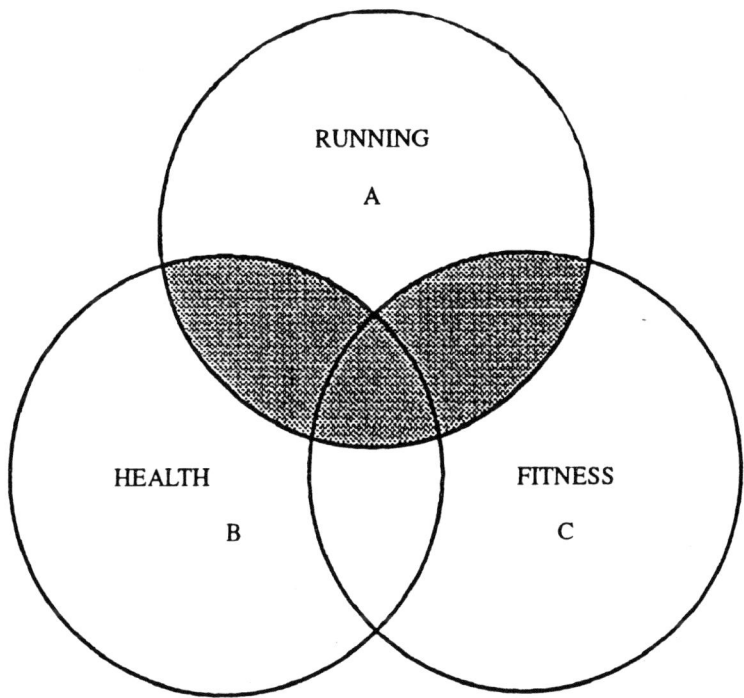

overlaps Circles B and C represents the records retrieved–the records containing the terms running and either health or fitness.

The result is a set consisting of all items that contain the terms running and health plus those items that contain the terms running and fitness. This technique of connecting a primary term with several analogous terms is one that you will see used over and over again in many variations. In ondisc searching the tendency to expand or broaden searches is almost irresistible.

The following record is one of the 13 records obtained by the request for **Running AND (Health OR Fitness)** in the ondisc database AUSPORT.[1]

---

1. Reprinted with permission from AUSTROM.

TITLE	Walking versus running in the conditioning of Australian army
AUTHOR	Rudzki, S. Australian Sports Medicine Federation. National Scientific Conference (25th : 1988 : Sydney, N.S.W.).
SOURCE	In, Torode, M., ed., The athlete maximising participation and minimising risk, Sydney, Cumberland College of Health Sciences, 1988, p. 59-61.
LANGUAGE	Eng
PUB. TYPE	Monograph chapter
LEVEL	Intermediate
DESCRIPTORS	army ; physical fitness ; walking ; running ; aerobic capacity ; comparative study
CALL NUMBER	AAIS

SEARCHING TECHNIQUES

A number of searching techniques can be applied to an ondisc search to achieve higher recall or to effect greater precision in the search. Some of the basic methods are explained below.

Brackets

Brackets are used within a search statement to control the order in which the search operators are used. The basic rule is that those terms and operators within brackets will be used first:

Fish AND Trout OR Perch

The above search without the use of brackets would not produce the result set that you would expect. It would retrieve those records containing the terms *fish* and *trout*, plus all records containing the term *perch*. To retrieve a meaningful result you must control the order in which the records are searched:

Fish AND (Trout OR Perch)

The above request *would* answer your search need because you would retrieve all records containing the term *fish* provided that the record also contained either the term *trout* or the term *perch*. Since the brackets control the search order, the search in Figure 6 would retrieve exactly the same results.

FIGURE 6. (Trout **OR** Perch) **AND** Fish

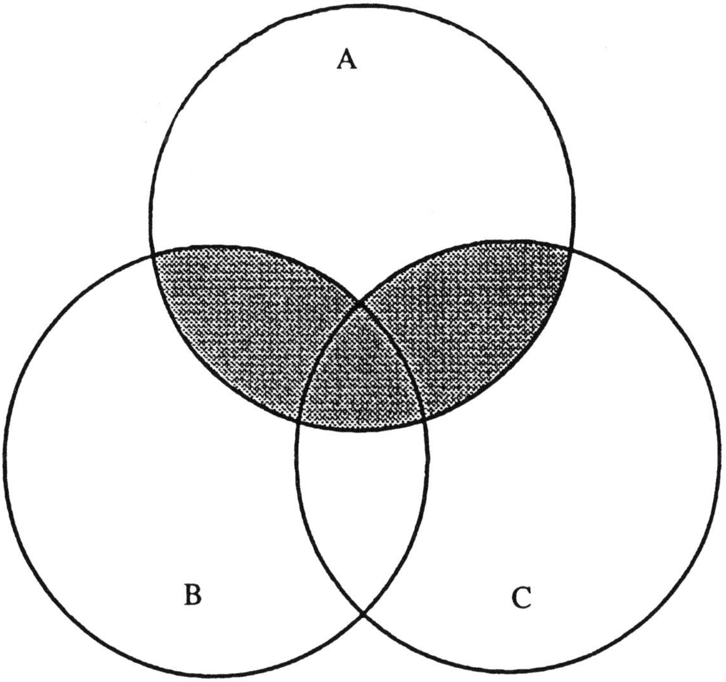

In the above illustration, A = Fish, B = Trout and C = Perch.

Controlled Vocabulary

Controlled vocabulary searching is possible in most major databases. It is accomplished by first using the database's thesaurus. The thesaurus may exist either in print form or as part of the CD ROM product. In either case, you will start by looking up your initial subject term in the thesaurus. The thesaurus will then provide you with the controlled vocabulary term that is used by that database. For example, if you are looking for information about the psychology of behavior in employees and how to modify employee behavior and attitudes, you would typically start by looking up the phrase Behavior Therapy in the thesaurus of Psychological Index Terms. In this case, you would find the following:

Behavior Therapy

    SN   Psychotherapeutic approach which employs classical conditioning and operant learning techniques in an attempt to eliminate or modify problem behavior, addressing itself primarily to the client's overt behavior, as opposed to thoughts, feelings, or other cognitive processes.

    B   Behavior Modification
    N   Aversion Therapy
          Implosive Therapy
          Reciprocal Inhibition Therapy
          Systematic Desensitization Therapy
    R   Behavior Contracting ∧ R

          Counterconditioning
          Paradoxical Techniques
          Psychotherapy
          Rational Emotive Therapy

In the above example, SN stands for Scope Note. The Scope Note gives you a brief description of the term's usage. The **B** stands for Broader terms. Broader terms are less precise, and give a more general coverage of the subject. The **N** stands for Narrower terms. Narrower terms are more precise and will help you target your search specifically. The **R** stands for Related terms. Related terms are subject terms that cover similar but distinct subject areas. Related terms, when they are applicable, should be used in addition to the initial terms/phrases.

Truncation

Truncation is the procedure that allows you to search on the trunk, or stem section of a term. It is important to be cautious with the use of truncation to avoid retrieving irrelevant material.

The following examples show how truncation may be used effectively.

Child*	will retrieve	Child
		Childs
		Children
		Childhood
		Children's
Run*	will retrieve	Run
		Runs
		Running
Play*	will retrieve	Play
		Player
		Plays
		Playing

The asterisk (*) is one of several common truncation operators. Other common operators include the dollar sign ($), the question mark (?) and the hash symbol (#). The truncation operator is product-specific and you will need to determine the one used by each product.

Combining Terms

The Boolean operator **OR** may be used as an alternative to a truncation operator when more control is sought. For example, look at the following:

Play OR Player OR Plays OR Playing

The above combination will retrieve the same result as would the truncation operator after the y in the word *play*. If you want a more specific result, you can pick and choose which variations on the word *play* you want to include in the search.

Look at the next example:

Play OR Plays OR Playing

The above combination, which uses the **OR** operator, would result in a more controlled and relevant search.

Proximity Operators

Proximity operators are similar to Boolean operators in that they are used to associate key terms or key concepts. Examples of proximity operators include the following:

With
Near
Same

The manner in which the above operators is used are product-specific. The operators must be used with considerable care since their use will effect a change in the result set. In Part II, proximity operators will be dealt with for individual products.

Stopwords

Stopwords are words that cannot be searched on. They may be words that have a special function such as the Boolean operators **AND**, **OR**, and **NOT**, or they may be words that are simply too common and of little subject value. For example, consider the following list:

the	they	of
a	were	by
to	when	from
this	who	was

The above list of stopwords is typical of the words that are too common and not usually available for searching in ondisc databases. Stopword lists will always be database-specific and you will need to check to determine which words are able to be searched.

Spelling

Spelling refers not only to the correct spelling of words/terms, but to the use of a spelling particular to the country that produces the database you intend to search. In most cases, American spelling is the most common and will accordingly yield a larger search result. For example, you will find a larger result set by searching on the term *color* than on the term *colour*. The following result is obtained by two searches on the PsycLIT database:

Color   758
Colour   263

It is important that you retrieve *all* of the relevant records that you are searching for, not just a large number of them. To retrieve records with variant spellings you should use the **OR** operator to ensure that each term is retrieved.

Field-Specific Searching

Field-specific searching is a technique that limits the searching to a specific field within the database record. Therefore it gives you more control in your search. Field-specific searching is second only to Boolean logic as an important strategy for your searching procedures. You will find, as you become familiar with a particular database and begin to acquaint yourself with the fields that make up its records, that your ability to target your search and retrieve relevant results will increase markedly.

As you become an experienced ondisc searcher you will realize that you are invariably searching a specific field whenever you undertake a search. As you practice searching, it is always a good policy to examine the records you retrieve to discover the fields that contain the terms you requested.

In the next chapter you will look at record structures and field-specific searching in greater detail. It is always important that you study your search results and that you are aware of the factors that may affect your result set.

SUMMARY

In this chapter you have been shown the basic techniques that allow you to accomplish the following tasks:

   a. Construct a search query by writing out your information need in the form of a question.
   b. Identify and isolate the keywords or key concepts from your initial query.
   c. Combine the key terms or key concepts to construct a search query.

The chapter went on to show you the control you can have when using the following techniques:

   a. Boolean logic
   b. brackets
   c. controlled vocabulary
   d. truncation
   e. proximity operators
   f. field-specific searching

The use of the above techniques will allow you to either *narrow* or *expand* your initial query. For example, consider the following list:

- Using the **AND** operator between two terms will *narrow* or *limit* a search to only those records which contain both terms.
- Using the **OR** operator between two terms will *broaden* or *expand* a search to include those records which contain either or both of the terms.
- Using the **NOT** operator between two terms will *narrow* or *limit* the search so as to exclude the second term from the record.
- Using **brackets** in a statement will enable you to control the order in which the search operators are used.

- Using **truncation** will *broaden* or *expand* a search to include those records which contain any variation of the stem or trunk term.
- Using **proximity operators** will allow you to associate terms with greater precision than is possible with **Boolean** operators.
- Using **field-specific searching** will *narrow* or *limit* the search to only those records which contain the requested term in the specific field indicated.

Figure 7 shows the steps involved in ondisc searching.

REVIEW QUESTIONS

1. Name the type of logic used in ondisc searching.
2. What will the result be when an **AND** operator is placed between two search terms?
3. What will the result be when an **OR** operator is placed between search terms?
4. Is it possible to use both an **AND** and an **OR** operator in the same search statement? If it is possible, why would you wish to do it?
5. What will be the result if a truncation operator is used after the stem of a word?
6. What alternative may you use in place of a truncation operator?
7. When would you want to use a **NOT** operator in a search statement?
8. Give three examples of stopwords and explain how they differ from other terms.
9. What would be the effect of using brackets in a search query?
10. Explain why you would use proximity operators in a search query and what effect they would have on your search outcome.

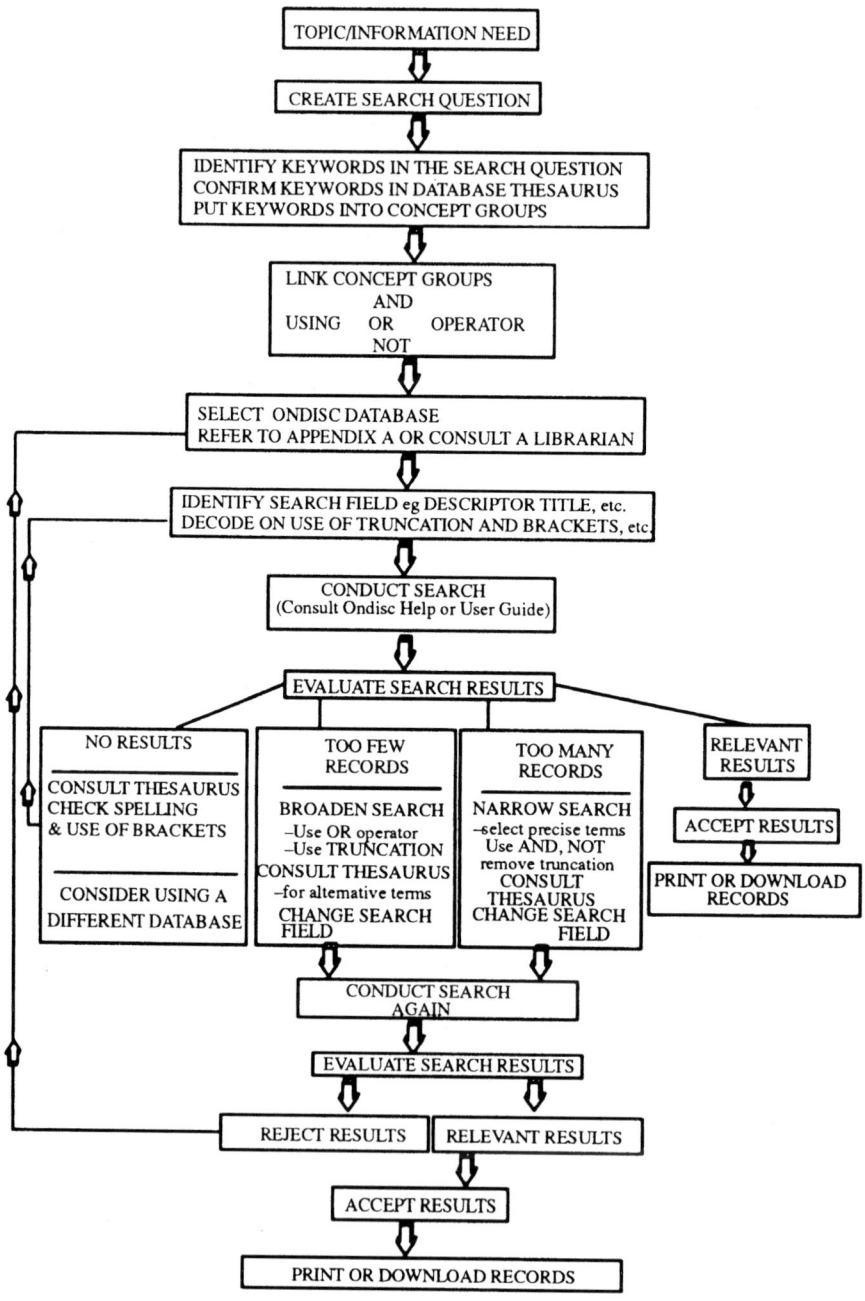

FIGURE 7. Steps in Ondisc Searching

Chapter 3

Record Structures

In this chapter you will examine the most basic component of the database, the *record*. You will see a demonstration of how knowledge of a database record structure can help you obtain the information that you are seeking. In the previous chapter you were introduced to basic searching strategies; in this chapter you will begin to apply those strategies to specific parts of the record.

RECORDS

The record is the major component of the database. Simply put, databases are made up of records, and a record is made up of fields. The fields are the data elements that make up the record. A bibliographic record will typically include a bibliographic citation, subject indexing terms (contained in the descriptor and identifier fields), and an abstract.

The type of record, then, will always correspond to the type of information that the database contains. Consider the following record sample from a database (ERIC)[1]:

AU: Schneider, Stephen H.
TI: The Changing Climate.
SO: Scientific American (v261 n3 p70-79 Sep 1989)
PY: 1989
AB:
    Discusses the **global change** of climate. Presents the trend of climate change with graphs. Describes mathematical climate

---

[1]. Reprinted with permission from OCLC

models including expressions for the interacting components of the ocean-atmosphere system and equations representing the basic physical laws governing their behaviour. Provides three possible responses on the change.

MJ:
Climate
Environmental Influences
Meteorology
Physics
Temperature
Thermal Environment

MN:
Climate Control
Higher Education
Mathematical Models
Science and Society
Science Programs
Scientific Research
Secondary Education
Soil Conservation

ID: Greenhouse Effect

The above record is obtained by a request for CLIMATE CONTROL IN **MN** (Minor Descriptor).

If you examine the above record sample, you can see the component parts of the record: fields. Each field has a purpose, and knowledge of a field's purpose will increase your ability to retrieve records and the documents to which the records refer. In the above example each of the fields has an abbreviation for its name (**TI** = title and **AB** = abstract, etc). If you examine the **MN** (minor descriptor) field, you will find the search phrase "climate control" that was sought in the above search. The fields **MJ** (major descriptor), **MN** (minor descriptor) and **ID** (identifier), will give you an additional selection of subject terms that can be used for subsequent searching. The terms found in the **MJ** and **MN** fields will typically be found in the databases thesaurus whereas the terms in the **ID** (identifier) field are added to increase subject access to the record.

Another field that is of particular note is the **SO** (source), as it is this field that will allow you to locate the item. In the above example the article is available from the journal, *Scientific American*, in the September 1989 issue, Volume 261, on pages 70-79.

FIELD-SPECIFIC SEARCHING

The above record, "The Changing Climate," is retrieved as an example of a field-specific search. This type of searching may be achieved in one or more fields. The advantage of field-specific searching is the control that it gives you over your search request.

In the above example, a search request is created containing the term "climate control." The search for these terms was conducted in the minor descriptor field. The abstract and title fields can be used to further enhance subject access to the record. The **PY** (publication year) field is often used to limit a search to either a single year or a range of years. The **PY** field will, in any case, inform you as to the year of publication.

RECORD STRUCTURES

The structure of records is always database-specific. You will find that the structure of records appears to be similar from one database to the next. This similarity can be misleading. The type of fields, the number of fields, and even the names of equivalent fields, will vary in different ondisc databases. The reason for the extent of the differences in record structure is that the records tend to reflect the nature of the data they contain. This difference is important to you because the fields that make up the record's structure are designed to enable you to retrieve records based on the database's content. That is, subject-specific fields are included to enable you to make precise distinctions among records based on a knowledge of the field's contents.

The records in the ondisc product PsycLIT contain a field that is unique to that database: the **PO** (population field). This field is used to identify the "population" or group that is being referred to in a particular record. The population may be animals, young adults, females, etc. The nature of the population that an article discusses will certainly affect the relevance of a particular group of records.

Until now, the fields you have considered have been searchable fields. It is common for databases to contain a number of fields that are not searchable. These fields are considered to have little subject value and are commonly used for administrative purposes in the organization of the database or to provide the record with a unique number.

The most productive search results will be achieved through a knowledge of the database's subject content and record structure, and will result from requests for information that are directed to specific fields. You are able to further enhance your control by combining Boolean logic with field-specific searches.

FIELD KEYS

The names of fields are frequently abbreviated. Below you will find some typical field abbreviations.

TI	Title
AU	Author
SO	Source
PY	Publication Year
AB	Abstract
MJ	Major Descriptors
MN	Minor Descriptors
ID	Identifiers
TE	Term
CO	Company

Knowledge of the record structure and its data components, fields, is part of the groundwork required for effective ondisc searching. In the above example **TE** (term) is the descriptor field for the database ABI/Inform, and **CO** is the abbreviation for company. In some other databases **CO** is used as an abbreviation for the code field.

Consider the example below of a field-specific search. In this example you will be seeking information about the company Dow Chemical and their activity in Canada. For this search you have selected the business database ABI/Inform. The key terms in the search question are **Canada**, the country/geographic region, and **Dow Chemical**.

The protocol for searching specific fields in ABI/Inform requires you to enter the keywords/phrases in the following manner at the **Find** prompt.

TE (Canada) and **CO** (Dow Chemical)

The following result was achieved:

Search Terms		
(01):	dow–DOW	217
(02):	chemical–CHEMICAL	552
(03):	(01) pre/1 (02)	136
(04):	canada–CANADA	9945
(05):	(03) and (04)	9

Search results in 9 item(s)

You will find, when you examine the records, that in each case the records will contain **Dow Chemical** in the **CO** (company) field, and **Canada** in the **TE** (term) field. This result is achieved because, in addition to your field-specific request, the Boolean operator **AND** was placed between the two requested keywords.

The following record is a sample from the above search for information on Dow Chemical in Canada.[2]

89-27883
Title: Sustainable Development
Authors: Buzzelli, David T.
Journal: Canadian Business Review (Canada) Vol: 16 Iss: 2
Date: Summer 1989
 pp: 22-24
Jrnl Code: CAB
ISSN: 0317-4026
Company: Dow Chemical Canada Inc (DUNS: 20-148-9580)

---

2. Reprinted with permission from UMI.

Terms: Canada; Case studies; Chemical industry; Social responsibility; Environment

Codes: 9170 (Non-US); 9110 (Company specific); 8640 (Chemical industry); 2410 (Social responsibility)

Abstract: The time is coming for Canadian businesses to clarify their views on environmental issues and the economy and to develop partnerships in industry, in the government, and in the community. Dow Chemical Canada Inc. has started to move in this direction. It has been taking an active interest in the school systems in the areas in which it operates. Dow Canada believes that public awareness is an important aspect of the educational component that is vital to the success of the concept of sustainable development. This concept recognises the need for economic growth to alleviate many environmental problems. Businesses need to show the public that they do care and that the environment is integrated into business and decision-making processes. Dow conducts a detailed environmental assessment of every project before it gets started. It also seeks out partnerships in the community. It has formed a community advisory panel in Sarnia on a hazardous waste facility. Tables. Graphs.

Another useful field-specific search that is common in literature databases is to retrieve a review of an item that has been written by a famous author. In any full record search for a famous author you are as likely to retrieve material written *about* the author's work as you are to find material written *by* the author.

For example, as a student you may wish to know what has been written by the author Peter Carey. Consider the following simple search:

FIND PETER CAREY

With the above search you would find every record with an occurrence of the name **PETER CAREY**, whether he was the author or the subject. To find only records of items that in fact, have been written *by* Peter Carey you would need to restrict the search to the author field. The procedure for doing this is, again, product-specific, but all products should allow you to do it. Basically, it would look like this:

FIND PETER CAREY IN AU

In the above example, **AU** represents the author field of a record. This search would retrieve only those records with an occurrence of **PETER CAREY** in the author field. You can also combine Boolean logic with field-specific searches. By using Boolean logic combined with field-specific searches you can begin to realize the true power available through ondisc searching.

For example, if you want information about a particular book written by Peter Carey, you could use the following search strategy:

FIND PETER CAREY IN AU AND ILLYWHACKER IN TI

In this example, **AU** again refers to the author field, and **TI** refers to the title field. The above search would retrieve every record with **PETER CAREY** in the author field and **ILLYWHACKER** in the title field. You need to be very careful when you conduct such searches to avoid missing relevant information. The reason for the concern is that you cannot be certain in what style or form Peter Carey's name will be used in the author field. For example, searching on the terms **PETER CAREY** would not retrieve records in which **P CAREY** is the entry used in the author field. There are two procedures that you can use to overcome this problem. The first approach involves the use of a Boolean operator, the **OR** operator; the second involves the use of a truncation operator. You may use either approach to avoid this problem, for example:

FIND PETER CAREY IN AU OR P CAREY IN AU AND ILLYWHACKER IN TI

The above search would retrieve every record that contains **PETER CAREY** in the author field, as well as those records that contain **P CAREY** in the author field provided the title is "**ILLYWHACKER**."

FIND P* CAREY IN AU AND OSCAR* IN TI

The * (asterisk) in the above search is used as a truncation operator. Common truncation operators, you will recall, include the asterisk * the question mark ?, the dollar sign $, and the hash # symbol. In the above example, the truncation operator is used in two ways. First, it is used to truncate **PETER** since it is not known how the author's first name is entered in the record. Truncation is used so that you can retrieve all records that contain either the **P** or **PETER** in the author field. Second, the truncation operator is used to truncate the title "Oscar and Lucinda" to enable you to retrieve the title by typing in its first word followed by the truncation operator. The ability to retrieve a title when only one or two words are known is frequently useful. Precise examples of field-specific searching will be used when you look at specific products.

Since you used a truncation operator, the above search will retrieve more records than the former example. This is because it would retrieve every record with **P** or **PETER CAREY** in the author field and phrases beginning with the word **OSCAR** in the title field. This means you may have also retrieved records that are not appropriate during the search, as you will have retrieved all phrases where the first letter in the author's name is **P**. For example, Paul would be retrieved. The amount of erroneous retrieval will still be limited by having **CAREY** in the author field and **OSCAR** in the title field.

SUMMARY

In this chapter you have been shown the basic components of the database record. You should now have an understanding of the following:

   a. The *Record* is the major component of the database.
   b. The components of the record, the fields, will be determined by the nature or type of information held in the database.
   c. These fields make up a typical bibliographic record.

   Title
   Author

Source
Publication Year
Abstract
Descriptors
Identifiers

d. The control that is provided by conducting *field-specific searches*.

REVIEW QUESTIONS

1. What do you call those data elements that constitute a record?
2. What type of search strategy, other than Boolean, could you use?
3. Are you able to search on combinations of fields? If so, give an example.
4. What is the purpose of the source field?
5. How does the descriptor field differ from the identifier field?
6. Why is it important to understand a record structure before you begin your search?
7. In the search for material on the greenhouse effect, find the fields in each record that contain the search terms.

Chapter 4

The Microcomputer

TYPES OF MICROCOMPUTERS

In this chapter the microcomputer will be explained in more detail. You will recall that in the first chapter the microcomputer was introduced as a major component of the CD ROM workstation. This chapter will also discuss the use of word processing software. The ability to incorporate your search results into a document or paper that you are preparing is one of the more productive outcomes of ondisc searching.

The microcomputer that you are most likely to encounter will be an IBM or an IBM compatible (an MS DOS computer). This would typically be a 286 or 386 level machine with a hard drive, a CD ROM drive, and one or more floppy drives. The difference between the 286 or 386 computer is the speed of access, the 386 being the quicker computer. Another important difference (to you) is the type or size of the floppy drive or drives.

Each floppy disc drive will be of one of two types: a 3 1/2" or a 5 1/4" disc drive. The difference does not end here. The drives may be either DD (double density) drives or HD (high density) drives. The 3 1/2" DD drive will format the disc to 720 K; the 3 1/2" HD drive will format the disc to 1.44 K. The 5 1/4" DD drive will format the disc to 640 K; the 5 1/4" HD will format the disc to 1.2 K. The difference between DD and HD drives is one of volume–the HD is able to store more data.

This may seem all too confusing. There are, however, some guiding rules for you to remember.

    a. A high-density drive can read a double-density disc.
    b. A double-density drive cannot read a disc formatted for high density.

This is important since one of the most useful outcomes of a search is the set of downloaded citations on your own floppy disc. You may find that the CD ROM station you are working at allows you to print citations. However, this is not common because most libraries are concerned about the cost of providing printing facilities, the noise caused by printing, the delay in searching caused by printing, and the ongoing maintenance that a printing facility requires. The workstation will invariably allow you to download the information to a floppy disc. This is a good practice in any case since the records can then be edited, sorted, and otherwise prepared prior to their eventual printing.

FORMATTING

You must format your disc prior to using it for downloading information. It is increasingly common for the discs that you purchase to already be formatted. It is essential that you either purchase formatted discs or format the disc yourself.

The procedure for formatting the disc is a simple one. It must be done with caution, however, for if you format a disc with information already on it, that information will be lost. In most cases you will be formatting new (empty) discs so that loss of information will not be a concern. If, however, you are formatting a used disc you will need to confirm that the disc is either empty or contains information that you no longer require.

A typical procedure for formatting a disc is given below:

1. Turn the computer on and let it start up fully.
2. Place the disc to be formatted in the appropriate drive (usually drive A, but possibly drive B), and close the drive door.
3. Type in the command **FORMAT A:** (if the disc is in drive A), and tap the **ENTER** key once.

The computer should then proceed with the formatting of your disc. If you encounter any difficulty at this stage, you should consult your DOS manual. When the formatting is complete the computer will ask you to name this volume. This is optional and not necessary in most cases. It will then inform you about the available space on the disc. This will take the form of two numbers: the top number is the amount of available space and the bottom number is the amount of actual space. These numbers should be the same if the format has been successful. If they are not the same, you should reformat the disc. If this is also unsuccessful, you are advised not to use that disc. The final question the computer will ask you is if you want to format another disc. If you *do* wish to format another disc, tap the Y key, remove the current disc and replace it with a new unformatted disc, and then tap the **ENTER** key. If you are finished, you only need to tap the **ENTER** key to finish the activity.

To confirm the amount of space available on your disc you can use the Check Disk command. To invoke the command you need to place your disc in the computer drive and then type in the command **CHKDSK** at the A prompt (provided your disc is in drive A). This command will allow you to discover the amount of space available on your disc.

To use your computer to its best advantage you should study your DOS manual and become acquainted with the DOS commands. While this is not essential it will save you a lot of frustration and give you increased confidence when you use a microcomputer.

THE KEYBOARD

The keyboard will be the major source of your interaction with the microcomputer and it is important that you understand the functions of various sets of keys.

The assorted searching software that you will encounter will each make different uses of the function or "F" keys. A particular command will be encoded into a specific function key. To use that command or activity, you will typically tap the function key once. The function keys are for the most part used by themselves, but occasionally they may also be used in conjunction with the **SHIFT**, **CTRL**, or **ALT** keys so as to provide another function.

In addition to the familiar alphabetical keys that are common to all products, other keys include the **arrow** keys, the **PgUp** (page up) and **PgDn** (page down) keys, and, *most importantly*, the **ENTER** or **RETURN** key. These keys are used for getting around in all of the products that you will be using.

The **CTRL**, **ALT**, and **DEL** keys have a special function; when they are pressed in unison, they reboot or restart the computer. You will, in time, use this procedure since it is occasionally the only avenue open to you. It is a serious procedure in that by doing it you will lose all search strategies and all searches that have not been downloaded to your floppy disc.

The keyboard is the means by which you communicate with the computer. The computer uses its screen to communicate to you. In searching ondisc you will find numerous menus available to assist you in your searching.

THE RESULTS

As mentioned above, you will be able to retrieve the results of your search in one of two ways. You can either download the search to a floppy disc or print the search.

Before you can print/download you will need to instruct the computer with regard to the number of records that you wish to print/download and whether you wish to print/download the entire record or only a portion of the record. To instruct the computer you will need either to "mark" the records that you wish to record or indicate the range of records (e.g., 1-10) that you intend to download. The details of this procedure are again product-specific and will be examined in detail in the product chapters.

DOWNLOADING

The expression "downloading" refers to the act of saving the result of your search to a floppy disc. This activity will enable you to take away the search and use it later. Results that have been downloaded may be either printed out directly or, as is recommended here, retrieved or uploaded into a word processing package.

Downloaded results will be sent (downloaded) as a file to your floppy disc. Because it is a file it will require both a file name and a file extension (for example, the name **sports.doc** where "sports" is the file name and "doc" is its extension). In an MS DOS system you are allowed to have up to eight characters in the file name and three characters in the file extension.

You are able to choose the name for the file that you create. This is important because the name must be recalled if you wish to retrieve the results of your search. All products will give a saved search a default name like **search.doc** but these default names are of little value as they give no indication of a search's content.

UPLOADING

Uploading is the process of retrieving your search results into a word processing document. All microcomputer-based word processors that run on an IBM or IBM compatible computer will allow you to retrieve your search results into a document. You will need to know the name of the file that you wish to retrieve and then enter the standard commands used to retrieve any document. The word processor will probably "convert" the document to the type that it would create. You may need to do some editing and layout work on the material in your document, but this is a small price to pay compared with the work that retyping involves. Uploading also reduces the potential for mistakes that exists when material is retyped.

The uploaded document may be used in the same manner as any document that you create by typing it in your word processing package. Throughout this text the word processing package WordPerfect will be used. The results shown in this work were initially downloaded to a floppy disc and later picked up or uploaded into the text. The main advantage of uploading your search is that it allows you to review your result sets and carefully select only those items that reflect your information need. You are also able to dress up your results and incorporate them into a document. This will be an extremely useful outcome if you are preparing a bibliography or a research paper.

MACINTOSH COMPUTERS

The products and hardware covered in this text refer to IBM or IBM compatible computers unless otherwise stated. However, the newer Macintosh computers can read or convert MS DOS (IBM-style) files so that they can be read and uploaded into word processing software that runs on your Macintosh. There is also an ever increasing number of ondisc products that can run the Apple Macintosh. This searching may be covered in a future edition of this text.

SUMMARY

In this chapter you have been shown the microcomputer in detail. You should have an understanding of the following:

   a. The type of computer you are most likely to encounter, the IBM or IBM-compatible 286 or 386 level machine.
   b. The difference between high-density and double-density drives.
   c. The two sizes of discs that are commonly used, the 3 1/2" and the 5 1/4" discs.
   d. The special function that the **CTRL**, **ALT**, and **DEL** keys have when they are pressed in unison, that this procedure allows you to "reboot" the computer.
   e. The caution you must take prior to "rebooting" since all information that has not been downloaded or printed will be lost.
   f. The procedure for *downloading* or storing the retrieved information to a disc.
   g. The procedure for *uploading* or retrieving information that has been stored on a disc.

REVIEW QUESTIONS

1. What component of the microcomputer do you use to communicate your question to the CD ROM workstation?
2. List the ways in which you are able to record the results of a search.
3. Explain the meaning of the term "download."
4. Why would you "reboot" the computer and why would you be cautious when using this procedure?
5. Which keys allow you to reboot the computer?
6. Explain the difference between downloading and uploading.

PART II:
PRODUCT-SPECIFIC SEARCHING

Chapter 5

DIALOG Ondisc Searching

DIALOG ondisc databases cover a wide variety of subjects. Each of the databases are provided as individual CD ROM products, with at least one CD ROM disc per database. The following databases are available ondisc from DIALOG.

SOURCES OF INFORMATION

Title	Coverage
Aerospace Database	1986-present
The Boston Globe	1986-present
Canadian Business & Current Affairs	1981-present
Corporate Affiliations	Current (reloaded quarterly)
Detroit Free Press	1988-present
DIALOG Bluesheets	Complete
Ei Chemdisc	1980-present
Ei Compendex Plus	1987-present
Ei Eedisc	1980-present
Ei Energy & Environment Disc	1980-present
Eric	1966-present
Federal Register	1988-present
Grants Database	Current (reloaded bimonthly)
Health Devices Alerts	1977-present
Healthcare Product Comparison System	Current
Idd M&A Transactions	1984-present
Kirk-Othmer Encyclopedia of Chemical Technology	Complete Third Edition

Title	Coverage
Los Angeles Times	1986-present
Medline	1984-present
Medline Clinical Collection	1986-present
Metadex Collection:	
Metals-Polymers-Ceramics	1985-present
Miami Herald	1988-present
Newsday & New York Newsday	1988-present
NTIS	1980-present
The Philadelphia Inquirer	1987-present
The Philosopher's Index	1940-present
Polymer Encyclopedia	Complete 2nd edition
San Francisco Chronicle	1987-present
San Jose Mercury News	1986-present
Standard & Poor's Corporations	Current year
Thomas Register	Current year
Trademarkscan-Federal	1984-present
Trademarkscan-State	1900-present

DIALOG is one of the most experienced database vendors and about the largest of the online database systems. The experience that DIALOG has in online searching is demonstrated by the excellent ondisc searching system that it provides.

Ondisc searching on the DIALOG CD ROM is available via two searching modes. The first searching method is an Easy Menu Search mode that allows you to select your search options from a variety of menus. The second searching method is the DIALOG Command Search which has commands based on DIALOG's online searching.

Searching DIALOG ondisc is extremely flexible and powerful since you are able to restrict your searches to any field or any combination of fields. All fields are searchable and any phrase or word may be connected with the use of an adjacency operator.

The examples given in this chapter will be taken from the Philosopher's Index ondisc. While the majority of examples will apply to most DIALOG ondisc products, some may apply specifically to the Philosopher's Index.

The Philosopher's Index

The Philosopher's Index database provides access to books and over 300 journals of philosophy and related fields of study. The database is produced by the Philosophy Documentation Center at Bowling Green State University. The print publication called "The Philosopher's Index" contains information that corresponds to the ondisc product. The major subject areas covered by the database include: Aesthetics, Epistemology, Ethics, Logic, Metaphilosophy, and Metaphysics. The Philosopher's Index covers, in addition to philosophy, philosophy in the disciplines of Anthropology, Education, History, Philosophy, Language, Law, Religion, and Science.

Easy Menu Search Mode

To start with the Easy Menu Search option you will need to highlight the Easy Search Option and tap the **ENTER** key. The next menu, entitled Select Main Activity, gives you the following options:

SELECT MAIN ACTIVITY

---

1) **Begin** a New Search (clears existing search)
2) **Database** Description Help
3) **Review** Search Helps
4) **Quit** Easy Menu Mode

To begin your search you will need to highlight the first selection from the menu and tap either the **ENTER** key or the highlighted letter (usually the first one) of the menu option. Selecting the first item from the menu will bring you to another menu that has the following options:

Search Options

---

1) Word/Phrase Index
2) Subject Headings

3) Title Words
4) Author Name
5) Journal Name
6) Named Person
7) Publication Year
8) Limit Options
9) Additional Search Options
10) Use Saved Search

The above menu options are important since they represent the various parts of the record you will search. The first option, the Word/Phrase Index, is a listing of all the words/phrases used in the database in alphabetical order. To use an option listed on the menu you need to highlight that option and tap the **ENTER** key. This action brings you to another screen where you are presented with a request to type in the first few characters of the term/phrase that you wish to search. This option is useful even if you know the terms/phrases that you wish to use because it will confirm their presence in the database and tell you the number of times the terms/phrases occur. The major limitation of using the Word/Phrase index is that it only allows you to search on a single term/phrase at a time.

The search options that immediately follow the Word/Phrase Index refer to specific parts of the record such as the **Subject field**, the **Author field**, and the **Title field**. An exception is the **Limit Options** (option 8) that allows you to restrict your search to only those items written in English, to those *not* written in English, and to the latest records that have been added to the database. The option **Additional Search Options** (option 9) is database-specific. Thus the contents of the Additional Search Options will differ from one database to the next. In the case of the Philosopher's Index, the following choice of searching options are provided:

> Words & Phrases
> Language
> Publisher
> Document Type
> Journal Announcement

The first of the additional options, Words & Phrases, is a type of free text search in that the abstract field and the title field are searched when this option is used. The remaining options are used to limit the search to a particular language, publisher, etc.

Boolean Searching
in the Easy Menu Search Mode

The Easy Menu Search mode allows you to use the Boolean operators **AND, OR,** and **NOT**. To use them you must select "Modify the current search with additional criteria" from the Select Main Activity menu. Selecting the Modify option will present you with the following menu:

Modify the Existing Search

Limit with additional concepts or terms
Include alternate terms
Exclude unwanted terms
Delete search steps

The first option shown in the above menu, "Limit with additional concepts or terms," is the direct equivalent of the **AND** operator. The additional concepts or terms will be linked to a preceding search by the **AND** operator. The second option, "Include alternate terms," is the direct equivalent of the **OR** operator. The alternate terms will be linked to the preceding search by the OR operator. The third option, "Exclude unwanted terms," is the direct equivalent of the **NOT** operator. The terms entered after selecting this option will be excluded from the original result set. The last option allows you to undo or delete unwanted search operations.

Care must be taken when using the above Boolean operators as you will be requested to use them in one of the record's fields. The selection of the appropriate field is essential for the Boolean operators to be used effectively.

Downloading and Printing in the Easy Menu Search Mode

The function key **F8** allows you to print or download your search results in the Easy Menu Search mode.

To begin, you must have the records displayed on the screen. Tapping the **F8** key at this point will cause the following menu to be displayed:

Adjust Options, then PRINT or TRANSFER

PRINT Currently Displayed Record Only
PRINT All _____ Selected Records
TRANSFER _____ Current Record Only to Disk
TRANSFER All Selected Records to Disk

Lines per page:
Page Break for Each Record:
Transfer File Format: DISPLAY

DIALOG Command Search Mode

The DIALOG Command Search mode is the more powerful of the two searching modes offered, and it will allow you to use both Boolean logic and field-specific searching to gain control over your search request. The use of field-specific searching is available for the major fields. The protocol for searching specific fields is based on a two letter abbreviation for each field. For the Philosopher's Index, the fields that you can restrict a search to include the Abstract, Descriptor, Title, Author, and Dialog Accession Number. The fields are used or accessed by either a suffix or prefix code:

SUFFIX CODES

/AB	AB	(ABSTRACT)
/DE	DE	(DESCRIPTOR)
/TI	TI	(TITLE)

PREFIX CODES

AN=   AN   (DIALOG ACCESSION NUMBER)
AU=   AU   (AUTHOR)

A suffix code must follow the terms/phrases in a request. For example, consider the following request:

RELIGION/AB AND TRUTH/TI

The above search request will retrieve only those records that contain the term **RELIGION** in the abstract field and **TRUTH** in the title field. When put into a search, the following results are obtained:

?SS RELIGION/AB AND TRUTH/TI

S1   1,962   RELIGION/AB
S2   1,857   TRUTH/TI
S3   30   RELIGION/AB AND TRUTH/TI
?

A prefix code must precede the terms/phrases in a request. For example, consider the following request:

?SS AU=JONES? AND AN>052017
S4   309   AU=JONES?
S5   2,000   AN>052017
S6   4   AU=JONES? AND AN>052017
?

The DIALOG Command Search is the second option on the Select Search Mode menu. To select this search mode you must highlight the search option and tap the **ENTER** key. This action will present you with a screen similar to the following illustration:

Philosopher's Index 1940 - (Current Year)

    Set   Items   Description
    ——— ——— —————

?

The above search screen is similar to the screen display that DIALOG offers for Online searching. The **?** (question mark) is the search prompt that DIALOG uses to indicate that a search query is required. You *must* precede each search request with a single S or SS. S refers to search and SS refers to super search. The difference between using the S prompt and the SS prompt is not in the search result but rather in the way the sets are organized. Consider the following two displays:

Display 1

? S ETHICS AND SCIENCE AND MEDICINE

	21,423	ETHICS
	21,547	SCIENCE
	1,390	MEDICINE
S4	86	ETHICS AND SCIENCE AND MEDICINE

?

Display 2

? SS ETHICS AND SCIENCE AND MEDICINE

S5	21,423	ETHICS
S6	21,547	SCIENCE
S7	1,390	MEDICINE
S8	86	ETHICS AND SCIENCE AND MEDICINE

The result sets for both of the searches are exactly the same. The difference is that set numbers have been attached to each of the terms/phrases in the second search. The attaching of set numbers to the terms gives you the added advantage of being able to search on any of the terms/phrases by using the set number. For example, consider the following search:

Display 3

```
? SS  S5 AND S7
S9      21,423    S5
S10      1,390    S7
S11        677    S5 AND S7
?
```

Set **S11** in the above example is a combination of the terms *ethics* and *medicine*. Using the set numbers instead of having to retype the terms/phrases is a shortcut that the Command Search mode allows on DIALOG.

Boolean Searching in the Command Search Mode

The Command Search mode allows full use of the Boolean operators **AND**, **OR**, and **NOT**. In the above example, ethics, science, and medicine were linked *using* the **AND** operator. In the following example the term *ethics, science,* and *medicine* will be used, but in this search the term *medicine* will be excluded from the result set. Note the difference in the result set.

Display 4

```
? SS ETHICS AND SCIENCE NOT MEDICINE
        S1  21,423    ETHICS
        S2  21,547    SCIENCE
        S3   1,390    MEDICINE
        S4   1,171    ETHICS AND SCIENCE NOT MEDICINE
?
```

The result in the above search is quite different from the previous search (Display 2): in the above example *medicine* is **excluded** instead of **included**. The number of records in the result set is larger in the second search because the number of records containing the term *medicine* is relatively small. Thus, only a relatively small number of records are excluded when the term *medicine* is *excluded* from the search. Alternatively, when a term such as *medicine*, with a small number of records, is included in a search (using the **AND** operator), the result set will be small.

You must remember, though, that the use of the **AND** or **NOT** operators will reduce the number of records retrieved. The use of the **OR** operator will increase the number of records that you retrieve. Consider the following search.

In this search you will again be seeking information on ethics in science. The concepts and search terms will need to be identified.

Concept 1 ETHICS   Concept 2 SCIENCE

The terms *ethics, science,* and *morality* will be included, and the term *medicine* will be excluded.

The Command Search mode allows you to include all of the above in your search statement and still obtain individual sets for each search term. To obtain the individual sets you will need to use the SS search command.

Display 5

?SS SCIENCE AND (ETHICS OR MORALITY) NOT
   MEDICINE

    S1 21,547 SCIENCE
    S2 21,423 ETHICS
    S3   5,452 MORALITY
    S4   1,390 MEDICINE
    S5   1,424 SCIENCE AND (ETHICS OR MORALITY)
                NOT MEDICINE
?

As the result set in the above search is still very large (1,424 records), this is a good opportunity to further refine your search.

The search request–your need for information–can be examined and refined. Are there particular areas of the study of science that are more relevant than others? One of the greatest benefits of ondisc searching is the freedom to modify your searches continuously. It not only helps you with a specific search request but also allows you to test and explore methods of retrieval.

Another alternative that you must always keep in mind is Controlled Vocabulary Searching through the use of a thesaurus and the record's descriptors field. Consider the following search request, with two specific aspects of science, psychology and sociology, in place of the more general term science. Note that the following search is conducted in the descriptors field.

?SS (PSYCHOLOGY/DE AND SOCIOLOGY/DE) AND
     (ETHICS/DE OR MORALITY/DE) NOT MEDICINE
S1 13,359   PSYCHOLOGY/DE
S2   1,280   SOCIOLOGY/DE
S3 19,433   ETHICS/DE
S4   3,691   MORALITY/DE
S5   1,390   MEDICINE
S6   15   (PSYCHOLOGY/DE AND SOCIOLOGY/DE)
              AND (ETHICS/DE OR MORALITY/DE) NOT
              MEDICINE
?

In the above example the search has been successfully refined. It is not always necessary or even desirable to reduce or refine a search to the extent where relevant records are excluded. Still, you will want to manage the result and make efficient use of the records you retrieved. The use of the field restricter **DE** in the above example will ensure that the records retrieved are relevant to the terms searched.

Sorting records into a meaningful order is a useful approach to organizing records you have retrieved. DIALOG ondisc allows you to sort records by title, author, journal name, publication year and frequency of search terms.

The following three records have been retrieved from the previous search request. Examine them for the terms you requested.[1]

1 of 15
165424

THE PURSUIT OF VIRTUE: THE UNION OF MORAL PSYCHOLOGY AND ETHICS.
Author: ARNOLD, BARRY
Publisher: NY LANG 1989
Language: ENGLISH
Document Type: MONOGRAPH
Journal Announcement: 233
THIS BOOK IS A MORAL PSYCHOLOGICAL AND ETHICAL RESPONSE TO ALASDAIR MACINTYRE'S "AFTER VIRTUE." UTILIZING THE CONTRIBUTIONS OF DAVID HUME AND OTHERS, THE AUTHOR INTEGRATES MORAL PSYCHOLOGICAL AND ETHICAL THEORY AS A POSITIVE CORRECTIVE TO MACINTYRE'S ARISTOTELIAN CRITIQUE OF MODERNITY. THE RESULT IS A PURSUIT OF VIRTUE WHICH IS NOT SQUELCHED BY THE ARCHENEMIES MACINTYRE IDENTIFIES AS EMOTIVISM AND EXISTENTIALISM. THE EVIVIFYING OF HUME'S PASSIONS WITH MODERN ANALOGUES IN SUCH THINKERS AS H R NIEBUHR AND GERARD GILLEMAN PROVIDES THE UNIQUE MATRIX FOR RAPPROCHEMENT AMONG PHILOSOPHY, PSYCHOLOGY, AND RELIGION. SUCH RAPPROCHEMENT PROFFERS A MOST PRODUCTIVE, INTEGRATED PURSUIT OF VIRTUE.
Descriptors: ETHICS; MORAL PSYCHOLOGY; VIRTUE; THEOLOGY; HISTORY; SOCIOLOGY
Named People: MACINTYRE, A; HUME; NIEBUHR, H; GILLEMAN, G

2 of 15
064468

---

1. Reprinted with permission from DIALOG.

UNITY OF PLAY: DIVERSITY OF GAMES.
Author: CAILLOIS, ROGER
Journal Name: DIOGENES, 19,92-122   FALL 57
Language: ENGLISH
Document Type: JOURNAL ARTICLE
Journal Announcement: RI2
Descriptors: ETHICS; GAME; PSYCHOLOGY; MATHEMATICS; SOCIOLOGY; PLAY; CHILDREN; RULE; CULTURE; CHANCE; GAME THEORY; GAMBLING
Named People: CHATEAU, J

3 of 15
002259

ETHICAL FUNCTIONS AS EFFECTS OF INDIVIDUAL AND GROUP PATTERNS.
Author: OPLER, MARVIN K
Journal Name: PHIL PHENOMENOL RES,   22,528-536   JE 62
Language: ENGLISH
Document Type: JOURNAL ARTICLE
Journal Announcement: RIP
Descriptors: ETHICS; IDEAL; RELATIVISM; PSYCHOLOGY; INDIVIDUAL; TEXT; CULTURE; SOCIOLOGY

TRUNCATION

The use of truncation to control your search result is a well-developed feature of the DIALOG ondisc products. The basic purpose of a truncation operator is to allow for a specific *trunk* or *stem* to be searched for, with an infinite number of possible "tails" limited only by the term's stem. For example, a search on the abbreviated term **TECHN?** would produce a large number of possible outcomes:

Technical
Technique
Techniques
Technocracy

Technocrat
Technocratic
Technocrats
Technology

Unfortunately a large number of the terms retrieved would be totally useless as **TECHN** is too brief or common a stem to produce a meaningful outcome. The truncation operator, the question mark ?, may be controlled more precisely within DIALOG.

To limit the number of terms to a single character following the truncation operator, you may leave a space and repeat the operator. For example,

ART? ?

Would retrieve only a single additional character following the stem **ART** thus arts would be retrieved and artist would not be retrieved.

The truncation operator may also determine the maximum number of characters following a stem. For example,

PAINT??

Would limit the number of characters following the stem to a maximum of two.

One of the most useful ways to use the truncation operator (?) is as a wildcard character. This means that you may insert the character within a term. For example,

M?n

Will retrieve both the terms man and men. You should recall that the **OR** operator may be used to determine precisely what terms you retrieve. Therefore, if you know the terms you intend to retrieve, you should use those terms linked by the **OR** operator. For example,

MAN OR MEN

DOWNLOADING AND PRINTING IN THE COMMAND SEARCH MODE

Downloading and printing are accomplished through a command at the ? prompt. A number of predefined record formats are available for downloading/printing information:

Format 1 DIALOG Accession Number

Format 2 Full Record except Abstract

Format 3 Bibliographic Citation

Format 4 Abstract and Title

Format 5 Full Record

Format 6 Title

Format 7 Bibliographic Citation and Abstract

Format 8 Title and Indexing

Format H Field containing retrieved terms (or "hits")

Format K KWIC (Key Word in Context) displays a window of text; may be used with other formats

Format T Title List only (no record headers)

The commands used for Downloading/Printing must include the following elements:

1. the set number that you wish to download from (e.g., S3)
2. the format number (to indicate the fields of the record)
3. the record numbers or range of records that you wish to download.

For example,

"**? Print S3/5/1-10**"

In the above print statement, **S3** is the set number, **5** is the format code and **1-10** is the range of records that you have nominated to print.

The procedure for downloading is the same as the procedure for printing except that you must use the Set command prior to downloading. The Set command will allow you to nominate the location (disc drive) and the file name. For example,

"? Set Print A:Educat.doc "

The above Set command will cause your print requests to be directed to drive A and the file to be called **Educat.doc**.

Chapter 6

SilverPlatter Ondisc Searching

In this chapter you will learn the basics of SilverPlatter's searching protocol on two of the most popular databases that SilverPlatter supports: the PsycLIT and SocioFile databases.

SilverPlatter is one of the most popular ondisc systems and many of the major databases are available through SilverPlatter. The main advantage of SilverPlatter is their well-developed searching software, *SPIRS,* that offers both the beginner and the advanced searcher the opportunity to conduct effective searches.

SOURCES OF INFORMATION

The following are some of the databases available on SilverPlatter:

AGRICOLA–an agricultural database
AGRIS
AV-ONLINE
BIOGRAPHICAL ABSTRACTS
CAB ABSTRACTS
CANCER-CD
CHEM-BANK
CIRR–Corporate & Industry Research Reports
CLAIMS/PATENT CD
CRIS
CROSS-CULTURAL CD
ECONLIT
EINECS
ERIC

LISA
MATHSCI DISC
MEDLINE
NTIS
NURSING & ALLIED HEALTH (CLINMED-CD)
OSH-ROM
PETERSON'S COLLEGE GUIDELINE
POPINE
PSYCLIT
SOCIOFILE
SPORT DISCUS
TOXLINE
TROPAC & RURAL

As you will note from the above list, SilverPlatter is one of the most comprehensive ondisc vendors and is a host for databases in a wide variety of subject areas.

SilverPlatter searching supports the types of search control that you have dealt with in the earlier chapters: Boolean searching, field-specific searching, and the use of truncation operators.

PsycLIT DATABASE

The PsycLIT database ondisc is an index to the world's periodical literature in psychology and related disciplines. PsycLIT, based on Psychological Abstracts, is the most comprehensive and respected database available in psychology. Psychological Abstracts are the print equivalent of PsycLIT ondisc. PsycLIT indexes over 1,450 journals from over 50 countries, in approximately 30 languages.

Record Structure

A record in PsycLIT will typically contain the following fields:

FIELD Names

Title
Author

Institution
Journal Name
Code
ISSN
Language
Publication
Abstract
Key Phrase
Descriptors
Classification Code
Population
Age Group
Update
Accession No.

Thesaurus of Psychological Index Terms

PsycLIT provides a thesaurus of terms/phrases that can be used in subject searching. The terms used in the PsycLIT thesaurus will be found in the descriptor field of the record. The PsycLIT thesaurus contains approximately 4,500 subject terms which are used to index the articles whose citations and abstracts are in the PsycLIT database. The thesaurus contains the cross references Use, Used for, Broader, Narrower, and Related Terms/Phrases. For example, let's look at the phrase "Psychosocial Development" as an entry in the thesaurus:

Psychosocial Development

SN	Process of psychological and social maturation occurring at any time during the life cycle.
B	Psychogenesis
N	Childhood Play Development
	Personality Development
	Psychosexual Development
R	Aging (Attitudes toward)
	Emotional Development
	Moral Development
	Object Relations

SN = Scope Note–explains briefly the way the term/phrase is used.
B = Broader Term–refers to more general or less specific terms/phrases.
N = Narrower Term–refers to more specific terms/phrases.
R = Related Term–refers to equivalent terms with similar meanings.

The alternative to searching for subject terms in the descriptor field (controlled vocabulary searching) is free text searching. Free text searching is searching using terms/phrases that are not taken from the controlled vocabulary of the thesaurus. The fields that you would search for FREE-TEXT include the Title Field (**TI**), the Key Phrase/Identifier Field (**KP**), and the Abstract Field (**AB**).

Ondisc Thesaurus

PsycLIT also provides an ondisc thesaurus of terms. The thesaurus option may be selected from the main menu. To select the option, you will need to tap the **T** key once. You will now be presented with a screen that requests you to type in the term that you wish to look up in the thesaurus. Once you have typed in the term, tap the **ENTER** key once to finish the operation.

If the term is suitable, tap the **S** key to select it and, finally, tap the **F** key to search for the term. Since the term being searched is located via the ondisc thesaurus, it will only be sought in the record's descriptor field.

SEARCHING ON SilverPlatter-PsycLIT

To begin searching on SilverPlatter you will need to type in your search at the Find prompt. Searching on SilverPlatter is very easy and very flexible. In each case you will begin your search from the Find prompt. The Find is one of the commands available from the main menu that is available across the bottom of the screen. To access the main menu, you need to tap the **ESCAPE** key once. To use any of the options offered by the main menu, you need to tap the highlighted letter.

A simple search might begin as follows:

FIND Dream*

In the above example you typed in the term **DREAM*** at the Find prompt and tapped the **ENTER** key to start the search. This would be followed by the PsycLIT database being searched for each occurrence of the term *dream*. The result is the creation of a set consisting of the records that contain the term *dream*.

The above request also illustrates how a truncation operator may be used. The use of the asterisk (*) after the **m** in *dream* will allow you to retrieve all variations of the term *dream* (i.e., dreams, dreaming, dreamed, etc).

No.	Records	Request
#1:	1163	DREAM

To display the above set you would need to tap the **F4** key. You are able to move within the record using the up and down arrow keys and from record to record using the **PgUp** and **PgDn** keys.

It is rare that a search will simply concern only a single term/phrase. It is much more common for a search to contain two or more concepts. For example, if you are seeking information on the meaning of color in dreams, you will need to divide the request into its basic concepts. Clearly, the two concepts in the request are the activity Dream (Concept 1) and the role of Color in dreams (Concept 2).

Boolean Searching

The OR Search

Consider the following example:

Color OR Colour in De

No.	Records	Request
#2	1419	(COLOR OR COLOUR) IN De

Color OR Colour (concept 2)

The above request is an example of how the **OR** operator may be used. The use of the **OR** operator here is interesting for, instead of using the **OR** operator to select similar terms/phrases, it provided a search on two terms with exactly the same meaning: the American spelling of the word *color* and the British spelling of the word *colour*. When you are searching international databases it is important to be aware of alternative spellings for the same word. The **OR** operator is useful in this instance.

In the above example, a field-specific limiting operator was used in addition to the **OR** operator. The operator **IN** was used to limit the search to only those records that contained either *color* or *colour* in the **Descriptor Field** (De). The descriptor field is the main subject field in the record, and terms located in the descriptor field may be found in the database thesaurus.

The AND Search

To search using the **AND** operator, you need to type the operator **AND** between your search terms/phrases, For example, to retrieve information on your concepts Dreaming **AND** Color, you will need to link the sets you created above with the **AND** operator:

#1 AND #2 (#1 = Dreams*), (#2 = Color OR Colour IN De)

No.	Records	Request
#1	846	Dream* IN De
#2	1419	(Color OR Colour) IN De
#3	5	#1 and #2

In the above example, set #1 (Concept 1) was linked by the **AND** operator with set #2 (Concept 2) to form your result set. If you examine the above result set, you will note the dramatic reduction in the number of records after the **AND** operator was introduced. The **AND** operator has this limiting effect in that it retrieves only those records that contain *both* of the requested terms.

If you examine the records shown below, you will note that in each case the terms *Dream* and *Colour* or *Color* will be found in the descriptor field. The following three records are examples of records from the result set #3.[1]

1 of 5
TI: Color in dreams and the psychoanalytic situation.
AU: Patalano,-Frank
IN: St John's U, NY
JN: American-Journal-of-Psychoanalysis; 1984 Sum Vol 44(2) 183-190
CO: AJPYA8
IS: 00029548
LA: English
PY: 1984
AB: Reviews research on the incidence and interpretation of spontaneously reported color elements in the dreams of psychoanalytic patients and discusses the hypothesis that spontaneously reported color dreams often represent the ego's attempts to work through, assimilate, and synthesize previously repressed material that has begun to surface in the course of psychoanalysis. In recognizing the emergence of previously inaccessible, tension-arousing material, the ego reacts with an affective signal–the color element in the dream. Colors in dreams have been held to represent a variety of phenomena, including childhood perceptions of the genitals of adults and children, disguised visual perceptions of body parts not usually seen, or repressed anal excremental contents. It has been asserted, however, that the anal significance of color only partly explains its presence and that color is often emblematic of the differences between body surface and body contents. Color serves a complex multiple function, determined and influenced by structural conflicts and the ongoing interplay among the id, ego, and superego. The ego utilizes color in the dream to camouflage and communicate material that has been hypercathected. It is suggested that the patient's color dream is a vivid example of the continuation of the working through process, in

---

1. Reprinted with permission from SilverPlatter.

which the ego attempts to assimilate fully previously fended-off aspects of mental life. The color dream of a 39-yr-old male psychoanalytic patient is described as an example of the workings of these mechanisms. (24 ref) (PsycLIT Database Copyright 1985 American Psychological Assn, all rights reserved)
KP: color in dreams; psychoanalytic patients
DE: COLOR-; PSYCHOANALYSIS-; DREAM-ANALYSIS; ADULTHOOD-
CC: 3310; 33
PO: Human
AG: Adult
UD: 8503
AN: 72-07253
JC: 1051

2 of 5
TI: The use of color for the secondary elaboration of the dream.
AU: Yazmajian,-Richard-V.
JN: Psychoanalytic-Quarterly; 1983 Apr Vol 52(2) 225-236
CO: PSQAAX
IS: 00332828
LA: English
PY: 1983
AB: Uses the term "secondary elaboration" to indicate the process by which further dream modification occurs after dream recall in order to deepen the disguise of the manifest content for the analyst. Clinical cases demonstrate the sole use of color for the alteration of dreams subsequent to their initial recall. Secondary elaboration in these cases is attributed to resistance to transference. The clinical material indicates that the secondary elaboration simultaneously serves a communicative function. (12 ref) (PsycLIT Database Copyright 1984 American Psychological Assn, all rights reserved)
KP: use of color for alteration of dreams subsequent to initial recall; resistance to transference; psychoanalytic patients
DE: DREAM-ANALYSIS; DREAM-CONTENT; COLOR-;

PSYCHO-THERAPEUTIC–TRANSFERENCE; PSYCH-THERAPEUTIC-RESISTANCE; ADULTHOOD-
CC: 3310; 33
PO: Human
AG: Adult
UD: 8401
AN: 71-01951
JC: 1622

3 of 5
TI: Color in the dreams of the color-blind.
AU: Yazmajian,-Richard-V.
JN: Psychoanalytic-Quarterly; 1982 Vol 51(3) 390-404
CO: PSQAAX
IS: 00332828
LA: English
PY: 1982
AB: Illustrates, using case studies, how 3 color-blind patients (aged 30-48 yrs) utilized color in their dreams in such a way as to actively deny their visual defect. Ss had displaced to the eyes some critical conflicts about other body parts. The use of color to deny color blindness further served to deny other physical defects, both real and imaginary. Additionally, this defence helped to fend off intense affects related to these defects as well as associated castration anxieties. (12 ref) (PsycLIT Database Copyright 1983 American Psychological Assn, all rights reserved)
KP: color content in dreams & role of denial; 30-48 yr old color blind patients
DE: COLOR-; COLOR-BLINDNESS; DENIAL-; DREAM-CONTENT
CC: 3290; 32
PO: Human
UD: 8303
AN: 69-06049
JC: 1622

The NOT Search

For the following example you will be seeking information about whether or not men are taking responsibility for birth control.

The first step you need to take is to identify the concepts that you want to include in your search strategy. You should also consider those concepts that you may wish to exclude. For example, two concepts emerge from the above question: Concept 1 (Birth Control) and Concept 2 (Men). A third concept that you may wish to exclude is not in the question but is, however, implied by the question. Concept 3 (Women) should be excluded from your search request.

The second step is to determine how to relate these concepts in a manner that will allow you to answer your question. In this case, you will need to use the **AND** operator to link Concept 1 (Birth Control) and Concept 2 (Men) and to use the **NOT** operator to exclude Concept 3 (Women).

It is useful to conduct your searches separately and introduce your logical connectors later. For example, with the above search, you will want to search first on the concept of Birth Control. This concept will be searched as a phrase. Your second concept (Men) can be searched by using the terms Men and Male with the **OR** operator, (i.e., Men **OR** Male). Likewise, your third concept (Women) can be searched using the terms Women and Female with the **OR** operator, (i.e., Women **OR** Female).

You have now developed your search strategy in a form that allows you to search. You need to consider what database is suitable for answering your request. For this question, two databases are likely candidates: PsycLIT and SocioFile. As both of these databases are available on SilverPlatter, the same search strategy can be used. For the example below, the PsycLIT database is used.

To begin your actual search, you need to type in the first phrase from Concept 1 (Birth Control in De) at the Find prompt. Note that the phrase Birth Control was requested only from the descriptor field. This limitation means that each record will have birth control as its main concern. The second search, Concept 2 (Men **OR** Male), can be usefully conducted as a single search statement with the **OR** operator between the two terms. Likewise, the third search, Concept 3 (Women **OR** Female), is conducted in the same manner.

You should retrieve the following result:

No.	Records	Requests
#1	313	Birth control in De
#25	54122	Men **OR** male
#3	45310	Women **OR** female
#4	11	(#1 **AND** #2) not #3

If you examine the sample records below, you will find that, in each case, *birth control* is in the descriptor field while *men* or *male* may be found anywhere in the record. However, the records will not contain the terms *women* or *female* since they are excluded in the search by the **NOT** operator.

The following two records are examples from result set #4 (in the above screen illustration).[2]

1 of 11

TI: Husbands' sex-role preferences and contraceptive intentions: The case of the male pill.
AU: Marsiglio,-William
IN: Ohio State U, Columbus
JN: Sex-Roles; 1985 Mar Vol 12(5-6) 655-663
CO: SROLDH
IS: 03600025
LA: English
PY: 1985
AB: Investigated the relationships among husbands' sex-role preferences, perceptions of contraceptive responsibility, and hypothetical intentions regarding the possible adoption of a male birth control pill. Data are drawn from a mailed survey of 49 husbands (mean age 30.6 yrs) during 1982 in Columbus, Ohio. Ss tended to be highly educated

---

2. Reprinted with persmission from SilverPlatter.

(57% were college graduates). Findings show that egalitarian sex-role preferences were moderately related to a greater stated likelihood of male pill usage for the sample as a whole and more strongly related for Ss not overly concerned with the chemical nature of a male pill. Modern sex-role preferences were also related to Ss' perception of contraception as a shared responsibility, although this perception was not related to the stated likelihood of male pill usage. (31 ref) (PsycLIT Database Copyright 1986 American Psychological Assn, all rights reserved)

KP: sex role preferences; perception of contraceptive responsibility & likelihood of male birth control pill usage; highly educated husbands
DE: HUSBANDS-; SEX-ROLE-ATTITUDES; FAMILY-PLANNING-ATTITUDES; BIRTH-CONTROL; ORAL-CONTRACEPTIVES; EGALITARIANISM-; ADULTHOOD-
CC: 2970
PO: Human
AG: Adult
UD: 8604
AN: 73-09069
JC: 2055

2 of 11

TI: The male role in contraception: Implications for health education.
AU: Chng,-Chwee-Lye
IN: North Texas State U, Div of Health Education, Denton
JN: Journal-of-School-Health; 1983 Mar Vol 53(3) 197-201
CO: JSHEA2
IS: 00224391
LA: English
PY: 1983
AB: Examines the available male contraceptives and discusses the implications of the changing male role in contraception for health professionals in the school and the community. It is concluded that despite the pill, the rate of unwanted pregnancies has grown substantially in the teenage population.

The growing involvement of men in contraception can make an important difference in these statistics. (23 ref) (PsycLIT Database Copyright 1984 American Psychological Assn, all rights reserved)
KP: role in contraception; males; implications for health education
DE: HUMAN-MALES; BIRTH-CONTROL
CC: 2970
PO: Human
UD: 8410
AN: 71-25798
JC: 1473

The same search on birth control can be conducted on a different database, SocioFile, to obtain a different slant or focus on the same topic. When this search was repeated on SocioFile, the following results were obtained:

No.	Records	Request
#1	462	Birth control in De
#2	12800	Men **OR** male
#3	19005	Women **OR** female
#4	14	(#1 and #2) not #3

The reason for reconducting the same search is to enable you to apply your search strategy to an alternative database. If you examine the records below, you will find that, while the topic is the same, the focus of the subject will tend to be different. For example, the records retrieved from PsycLIT should be more concerned with the individual's relationship to birth control, whereas the records retrieved from SocioFile should be more concerned with the social implications of birth control.

The following two records were retrieved from the SocioFile search's result set #4:[3]

---

3. Reprinted with permission from SilverPlatter.

1 of 14

- **TI:** Adolescent Males' Sexual Behavior and Contraceptive Use: Implications for Male Responsibility
- **AU:** Pleck,-Joseph-H.; Sonenstein,-Freya-L.; Swain,-Scott-O.
- **IN:** Dept Psychology Wheaton Coll, Norton MA 02766
- **JN:** Journal-of-Adolescent-Research; 1988, 3, 3-4, fall-winter, 275-284.
- **CO:** JADREZ
- **AVA:** Hard copy reproduction available from SA; document not on microfilm
- **DT:** aja Abstract-of-Journal-Article
- **LA:** English
- **CP:** United-States
- **PY:** 1988
- **AB:** Analysis of data from the 1979 National Survey of Young Men reveals that 17.1% of never-married metropolitan-area males (Ms) ages 17-21 reported using a condom at first intercourse, & almost the same proportion (15.5%) reported condom use at most recent intercourse; withdrawal was also frequently reported as a contraceptive method. Condom use was associated with being older at first intercourse, having higher actual or aspired education, having a closer relationship with the partner, & believing the M has sole contraceptive responsibility. At the same time, in their current sexual behavior, condom users tended to be younger, & not to believe in shared responsibility for contraception. These data may be interpreted as indicating that adolescent Ms abdicate responsibility for contraception as they become more sexually experienced. Alternatively, these data may show that condom use is developmentally a transitional phenomenon, & that M responsibility takes different forms later (as compared to earlier) in adolescent Ms' sexual experience. 4 Tables, 9 References. HA (Copyright 1989, Sociological Abstracts, Inc., all rights reserved.)
- **DE:** Metropolitan-Areas (D516900); Adolescents- (D008400); Birth-Control (D082800); Sexual-Behavior (D761400); Males- (D484200); Responsibility- (D715500)

IP:	contraceptive use/sexual behavior, adolescent males, responsibility issues; 1979 national survey;
SH:	the family and socialization; sociology of sexual behavior (1940)
CC:	1940; 1900
AN:	89V0521
AV:	SA

2 of 14

TI:	Male Involvement in Contraceptive Decision Making: The Role of Birth Control Counsellors
AU:	Scales,-Peter; Etelis,-Robyn; Levitz,-Norman
IN:	Instit Family Research & Education, Syracuse NY 13210
JN:	Journal-of-Community-Health; 1977, 3, 1, fall, 54-60.
CO:	JCMHBR
AVA:	Hard copy reproduction available from SA; document not on microfilm
DT:	aja Abstract-of-Journal-Article
LA:	English
CP:	United-States
PY:	1977
AB:	Reported is a participant-observation study of 7 family-planning agencies in a large Northeastern city which were investigated to discover the extent to which young men are encouraged by birth control counsellors to be involved in decision making about contraception. Results indicated that male involvement is only mildly encouraged; implications for sexual decision making & for social service agencies are discussed. 1 Table. HA
DE:	Contraceptive, Contraceptives, Contraception (114475); Decision-making- (122000); Male, Males (256635); Birth-control (055210); Counsel, Counselling, Counsellor, Counsellors (116380)
IP:	contraceptive decision making, male involvement; birth control counsellors' role; participant observation; family planning agencies, Northeastern US city;
SH:	demography and human biology; demography (population studies) (1837)

CC: 1837; 1800
AN: 81L9157
AV: SA

SPECIAL FEATURES

Field-Specific Searching

You are able to control a search by restricting that search to a specific field. The procedure for searching in a specific field with SilverPlatter is very straightforward. You need only request that the term be in the field of your choice. For example, **Jones** in **AU**, where Jones is the author that you are seeking and **AU** is the abbreviation for the author field.

The other control operators include the = (equal) operator (e.g., **la=english**, where English is the language you seek and la is the abbreviation for the language field). The > (greater than) operator and the < (less than) operator may also be used, typically with the publication year field. The abbreviation for publication year is PY. Therefore, searching on **PY > 1984** would retrieve only those records with a publication date greater than 1984. You are also able to search on a range of years. For example, requesting **PY=1984-1992** would only retrieve those records published between 1984 and 1992.

Lateral Searching

Lateral searching is a procedure that allows you to identify terms found within records you are reviewing and to search on those terms directly. The procedure begins by highlighting the term you intend to search by moving to it using the up or down arrow keys. Once the term is highlighted, you need to tap the **S** key to select it and then tap the **F** key to search for the term.

Marking Records

The ability to mark or tag records for later use is a valuable feature. It allows you to almost effortlessly identify records that you wish to save for later consideration, printing, or downloading. The procedure for marking a record is to tap the **M** key (an option from the main menu) while you are viewing the record that you wish to mark. A marked record will have * (asterisk) along the lefthand side of the record. The procedure to unmark the record is equally simple: you need only tap the **U** key (an option from the main menu) while you are viewing the marked record that you wish to unmark.

PRINTING RECORDS

Again, the print option is one of the options from the main menu. To begin the procedure you need to select the print option by tapping the **P** key once. This action will bring you to a screen that offers you a number of default options for printing. The menu asks you to either proceed with the printing (thus accepting the default options) or select **C** (to change or alter the default options). It is important to confirm that you are satisfied with two of the options before you proceed: the fields that you intend to print and the number of records that you intend to print.

The default option for the fields will have been set up by the library providing the service. You cannot assume that they have selected the option that allows you to print the entire record. Conversely, you may not wish to print all the fields and may, for example, only want to print the title and the source fields to conserve paper. In either case you are able to make the choice prior to printing.

The other important choice to make is about the records that you intend to print. The options include Marked Records, All Records, Current Record, and any nominated records. To nominate records you may simply type in the record's number (e.g., 15), select a range of records (10-15), or nominate various records (e.g., 1,7,10,15). The choice is yours. The best procedure is to mark the records and print the records that you mark.

DOWNLOADING RECORDS

The downloading procedure is similar to the print procedure. You must begin by selecting the download option from the main menu.

The most important difference between the two is that when you download you are given the opportunity to name the file that you wish to download to. This is an important option and one that you should do carefully because selecting a *meaningful* name will allow you to retrieve the document later. You also have the same responsibility to determine the fields that you wish to select and the records that you wish to download. With downloading you do not need to be as conservative with your selection as you do with printing. No paper will be wasted and floppy discs can always be reused. So, unless you are absolutely positive that you do not require a specific field, it is wise to download the entire record.

The download operation may be stopped by tapping the **CTRL** and **BREAK** keys simultaneously.

Chapter 7

WILSONDISC Searching

SOURCES OF INFORMATION

WILSONDISC databases cover a variety of subjects. Each of the databases is provided as a single CD ROM product. The following databases are available from WILSONDISC:

ART Art Index
AST Applied Science & Technology Index
BIO Biography Index
BPI Business Periodicals Index
CBI Cumulative Book Index
EDI Education Index
GSI General Science Index
HUM Humanities Index
ILP Index to Legal Periodicals
LIB Library Literature
RDG Reader's Guide to Periodical Literature
SSI Social Sciences Index

WILSONDISC products are updated quarterly and the additional information is cumulative.

The Databases in Detail

Art Index

ART The Art Index database ondisc provides information on the following: ARCHAEOLOGY, ARCHITECTURE, CITY PLANNING, DESIGN, MOTION PICTURES, MUSEUM STUDIES, AND PHOTOGRAPHY.

Applied Science & Technology

AST The Applied Science & Technology database ondisc provides information on the following: ENGINEERING, CHEMISTRY, MATHEMATICS, PHYSICS, COMPUTER TECHNOLOGY, DATA PROCESSING, AND TOPICS ON ENERGY.

Biography Index

BIO The Biography Index database ondisc provides information on the following: BIBLIOGRAPHIES, CRITICAL STUDIES, FICTION, DRAMA, POETRY.

Business Periodicals Index

BPI Business Periodicals Index database ondisc povides information on the following: ACCOUNTING, ADVERTISING, BANKING, CHEMICAL INDUSTRY, COMMUNICATIONS, COMPUTER TECHNOLOGY, COMPUTER APPLICATIONS, CONSTRUCTION INDUSTRY, DRUG AND COSMETIC INDUSTRIES, ECONOMICS, ELECTRONICS, FINANCE AND INVESTMENTS, INDUSTRIAL RELATIONS, INSURANCE, INTERNATIONAL BUSINESS, MANAGEMENT, PERSONNEL, ADMINISTRATION, MARKETING, OCCUPATIONAL HEALTH AND SAFETY, PAPER AND PULP INDUSTRY, PETROLEUM AND GAS INDUSTRIES, PRINTING AND PUBLISHING, PUBLIC RELATIONS, PUBLIC UTILITIES, REAL ESTATE, TRANSPORTATION, TRADE AND INDUSTRY, ASSOCIATION REPORTS, PRODUCT REVIEWS, STATISTICS.

Cumulative Book Index

CBI The Cumulative Book Index database ondisc provides information on the following: HARDCOVER FICTION AND NONFICTION, POETRY, PLAYS, JUVENILE LITERATURE, SCHOLARLY WORKS, REPRINTS, DICTION-

ARIES, FOREIGN LANGUAGE CLASSICS, PAPERBACKS OF 100 PAGES OF MORE.

Education Index

EDI   The Education Index database ondisc provides information on the following:

All levels of school:
ELEMENTARY, SECONDARY, AND HIGHER EDUCATION, TEACHER EDUCATION, TEACHING METHODS, SCHOOL ADMINISTRATION, PARENT-TEACHER RELATIONS, COUNSELLING.

Subject specific information:
SCIENCE, MATH, MUSIC, SOCIAL STUDIES, MULTICULTURAL EDUCATION, COOPERATIVE EDUCATION, HEALTH, PHYSICAL EDUCATION, LANGUAGE, RELIGIOUS EDUCATION, SEX EDUCATION.

General Science Index

GSI   The General Science Index database ondisc provides information on the following:

The physical sciences:
ASTRONOMY, ATMOSPHERIC SCIENCE, CHEMISTRY, EARTH SCIENCE, PHYSICS, OCEANOGRAPHY, AND MATHEMATICS.

The life sciences:
MEDICINE, HEALTH, BIOLOGY, MICROBOLOGY, ZOOLOGY, BOTANY, ENVIRONMENTAL STUDIES, CONSERVATION, AND GENETICS.

Humanities Index

HUM   The Humanities Index database ondisc provides information on the following: ART, LITERATURE, LINGUISTICS,

HISTORY, MUSIC, PERFORMING ARTS, PHILOSOPHY, RELIGION, THEOLOGY, AND FILM.

Index to Legal Periodicals

ILP   The Index to Legal Periodicals database ondisc provides information on the following:

All matters relating to law:
COPYRIGHT, LABOR, COMMERCIAL, CONSTITUTIONAL, INTERNATIONAL, CRIMINAL, PROPERTY, AND PROCEDURAL LAW.

Library Literature Index

LIB   The Library Literature index ondisc provides information on the following:

All aspects of librarianship:
INFORMATION RETRIEVAL AND STORAGE, ABSTRACTING AND INDEXING, BOOKS AND PUBLISHING, CHILDREN'S LITERATURE, ASSOCIATIONS, AND CONFERENCES.

Reader's Guide to Periodical Literature

RDG   The Reader's Guide to Periodical Literature database ondisc provides information on the following: CURRENT EVENTS, NEWS, POLITICS, BUSINESS, SCIENCE, EDUCATION, RELIGION, FOREIGN AFFAIRS, FASHION, SPORTS AND HOBBIES, HEALTH, NUTRITION, FOOD, AND COOKING.

Social Sciences Index

SSI   The Social Sciences Index database ondisc provides information on the following: ECONOMICS, POLITICS, SOCIOLOGY, PSYCHOLOGY, ANTHROPOLOGY, ENVIRONMENTAL STUDIES, URBAN STUDIES, FOREIGN AFFAIRS, PUBLIC HEALTH, PUBLIC ADMINISTRATION.

SEARCHING ON WILSONDISC

The WILSONDISC database used in the following examples is the Reader's Guide to Periodical Literature.

WILSONDISC is one of the easiest searching platforms for the beginning searcher as it offers a variety of searching modes. It is, however, difficult for the advanced searcher to use in a definitive manner since obtaining precise or consistent results can be difficult.

When you begin searching on WILSONDISC you are given a choice of three search modes:

   a. **BROWSE**
   b. **WILSEARCH**
   c. **WILSONLINE**

To begin the actual search you must start by selecting one of the above search modes. Selecting BROWSE will give you the most basic method of searching. To search with BROWSE, you begin by entering a search term. This action results in an alphabetic listing of terms that Wilsondisc uses to provide you with *subject* access to the citations that you are seeking instead of retrieving the articles directly. You are able to select the appropriate term and use it to locate the citations.

The Three Search Modes

BROWSE

Searching **BROWSE** is a basic approach that allows you to find the *subject terms* that are used in the Wilsondisc database. To begin, you must select the **BROWSE** option from the initial search menu and then type in the term/phrase that you intend to search on. For example, searching on the term *East Timor* retrieves the following list:[1]

ENTRIES	SUBJECT
2	EAST SAINT LOUIS(ILL.)/SPORTS
1	EAST SALINAS (CALIF.)/EDUCATION

---

1. Reprinted with permission from WILSONDISC.

1	EAST STROKE (ENGLAND)/HISTORIC HOUSES, SITES, ETC.
1	EAST TENNESSEE STATE UNIVERSITY
1	EAST TENNESSEE STATE UNIVERSITY/CENTER FOR APPALACHIAN STUDY
1	EAST TEXAS TELEVISION NETWORK
2	**EAST TIMOR (INDONESIA)/POLITICS AND GOVERNMENT**
*	EAST WOODS PRESS
*	EAST 14TH STREET BAND
1	EAST-WEST AIRLINES LTD.
7	EAST-WEST TRADE
1	EAST, NATHAN
1	EAST, SARITA KENEDY

The term that was searched on, *East Timor*, is highlighted and the articles relevant to that subject heading can be retrieved by tapping the **ENTER** key. The following two articles are samples of the records retrieved:[2]

1 RGA (Readers' Guide Abstracts)

Author:
Hertsgaard, Mark

Title:
The secret life of Henry Kissinger (minutes of State Dept. meeting discussing U.S. role in Indonesia's invasion of East Timor; cover story)

Source:
The Nation v251 p473+ October 29 '90 il

SUBJECTS COVERED:
Indonesia/Territorial expansion
East Timor (Indonesia)/Politics and government
United States/Foreign relations/Indonesia/History
Government and the press
Kissinger, Henry:1923-

---

2. Reprinted with permission from WILSONDISC.

ABSTRACT:

Former secretary of state Henry Kissinger has a record of keeping the American public and Congress in the dark about government actions. To indicate America's strength in the cold war, Kissinger signalled Jakarta in 1975 that the United States would not object if Indonesia invaded East Timor, an island located on the eastern end of the Indonesian archipelago that was controlled by the leftist Fretilin movement. According to church sources, the invasion resulted in the deaths of an estimated 100,000 people. In a State Department meeting that year, Kissinger revealed a disregard for the human consequences of his actions. He upbraided his associates for sending him a cable about U.S. policy in East Timor because he feared that the cable might be leaked to the press. Now that he is being cited as an expert on foreign policy with regard to the Persian Gulf crisis, it is important to remember his disdain for telling the truth. The minutes of the 1975 meeting are provided.

2 RGA (Readers' Guide Abstracts)

Author:
Nordland, Rod

Title:
Visiting a forgotten war (Pope John Paul II)

Source:
Newsweek v114 p38 October 23 '89 il map

SUBJECTS COVERED:
East Timor (Indonesia)/Politics and government
Indonesia/Territorial expansion
John Paul:II:Pope:1920-/Visit to East Timor (Indonesia), 1989

ABSTRACT:

For the past 14 years, little has been known about the devastating war being waged in East Timor. Predominantly Muslim Indonesia invaded the Catholic province in 1975, and it has since maintained harsh control over the territory. The Timorese have endured starvation, relocation, and incarceration in concentration camps at the hands of the Indonesians, and famine and war have killed nearly one-third of the population. Few people know of the violence because ruling Indonesians forbid foreign observers from entering East Timor and natives from leaving. The government recently opened its doors to some visitors in hopes of convincing outsiders that the war is over, but the province's graveyards reveal a different story. During a recent visit to East Timor, Pope John Paul II lent support to the cause of East Timorese Catholics and called for human rights safeguards.

Thus, with a very quick search on the term/phrase *East Timor* you were able to retrieve two articles on that topic. **BROWSE** is the most basic searching mode provided by WILSONDISC. In the next section you will be introduced to **WILSEARCH**.

WILSEARCH

The **WILSEARCH** searching mode is one of the most popular and useful methods of searching a WILSONDISC product. This method assists the searcher by providing a menu or form for the searcher to fill in.

For example, in Readers' Guide to Periodical Literature you are presented with the following screen:

Enter your local search request for RGA
Subject Words: **East Timor**
   2nd subject:
   3nd subject:

Personal name:
   Title words:

Journal name:
Organization:
Dewey number:

The above screen allows you to type in the terms that you wish to search on in the appropriate part of the record. Thus you would enter the subject term/phrase *East Timor* in the subject field. The other subject fields only need to be used when additional subject terms/phrases are used.

For example the above search on the subject of East Timor in **WILSEARCH** retrieved the following set:

FIND EAST (BI) AND TIMOR (BI)
        (BI) EAST. . . . 1372 Entries
        (BI) TIMOR . . . . . 4 Entries
    4 Entries

The above diagram/screen illustrates how **WILSEARCH** actually conducts your search. You create the search by typing **East Timor** in the first menu line, Subject Words. Yet, because you entered two terms, they are searched separately and then combined later with the Boolean operator **AND**. The term **EAST** was found on 1372 occasions and the term **TIMOR** was found on four occasions. Furthermore, when the terms were later combined, the combination of the two terms revealed that the term **EAST** was found on each occasion with the term **TIMOR** thus the final set number equals the set number found for the single term **TIMOR**.

The above search retrieved four records, of which the first two were the same that you retrieved earlier in the **BROWSE** search. The following two records were not previously located.[3]

3 RGA (Readers' Guide Abstracts)

Book Review:
Ramos-Horta, Jose
Funu ; the unfinished saga of East Timor
reviewed by Nossiter, Bernard D.
The Progressive v51 p42 March '87

---

3. Reprinted with permission from WILSONDISC.

SUBJECTS COVERED:
Revolutionists/Indonesia/Timor Timur/Biography
Timor Timur (Indonesia)/Politics and government
Ramos-Horta, Jose

4 RGA (Readers' Guide Abstracts)
Book Review:
Ramos-Horta, Jose
Funu ; the unfinished saga of East Timor
reviewed by Kamm, Henry
The New York Times Book Review v92 p26 January 11 '87

SUBJECTS COVERED:
Revolutionists/Indonesia/Timor Timur/Biography
Timor Timur (Indonesia)/Politics and government
Ramos-Horta, Jose

WILSONLINE

Searching via the **WILSONLINE** mode is still ondisc searching, though it closely resembles an online searching mode.
When you select the WILSONLINE searching option you are presented with the following screen:

Readers' Guide Abstracts   Data Coverage: 1/83 thru 01/24/91

SEARCH SET	WILSONLINE COMMAND	NUMBER of ENTRIES

USER:_____
F1:HELP F2:END F3:Change Database/Disc F10:Reshow last FIND/NBR

The above screen allows you to type in the terms that you wish to search on after the word **USER:**. It requires you to insert the Boolean operator that you wish to use. For example, the search for material on East Timor requires that you enter the search with the **AND** operator between the two terms.

EAST AND TIMOR

Searching in the above manner using the WILSONLINE mode retrieves the following results:

Readers' Guide Abstracts   Data Coverage: 1/83 thru 01/24/91

SEARCH	WILSONLINE COMMAND	NUMBER of ENTRIES
1 EAST AND TIMOR		**8**
	EAST . . . . . . 4254 Entries	
	TIMOR . . . . 8 Entries	

USER: EAST AND TIMOR

F1: HELP F2:END F3:Change Database/Disc F10:Reshow last FIND/NBR

The term *East* was found on 4254 occasions, and the term *Timor* was found on only eight occasions. Furthermore, when the terms were later combined, the combination revealed that the term *East* was found on each occasion with the term *Timor*. Thus the final set number equals the set number found for the single term *Timor*.

The above search retrieved eight records, four of which were the same that you retrieved earlier in the **BROWSE** and **WILSEARCH** modes. In addition, four new records were located as well. The above searches were conducted to illustrate that you cannot assume you will retrieve the same results by searching on the same term/phrase in each of the different search modes, even though the same database is being searched. The reason for this is that different parts of the database are being searched on each occasion. While the **WILSONLINE** search retrieves the greatest number of records, it is, in fact, the searching mode that gives you the most control.

Searching control is gained in two ways: either through the use of Boolean logic or through the use of field-specific searching. **WILSONLINE** allows you to restrict your search by using field-specific searches in the following ways:

SEARCH CATEGORY QUALIFIERS

(AU) Author, personal name
(BI) Basic Index
(CA) Author, corporate
(CS) Subject, corporate
(DS) Descriptor string
(JN) Journal name/abbreviation
(LA) Language
(PS) Subject, personal name
(SH) Subject heading
(TI) Title
(YR) Year of publication

The above qualifiers are the key to doing field-specific searching in the **WILSONLINE** search mode. The search qualifier always follows the search term in the following manner:

EAST TIMOR (BI)

The above example shows how a search for East Timor can be restricted to the Basic Index. Using the **(BI)** qualifier in the **WILSONLINE** mode, you retrieve the exact result set that was retrieved in the **WILSEARCH** mode. This occurs because **WILSEARCH** defaults to, and always searches in, the Basic Index mode **(BI)** for subject searches, unless another mode is qualified. You may choose to use any of the qualifiers, or even two qualifiers, provided they are used as above, that is, in brackets and following the search term.

DOWNLOADING AND PRINTING

The command that allows you to download is the same command that allows you to print. To start the process you must have completed your search and presented the records. At this point, tapping the **F4** key will present you with the following display:

Print Entry
Press **Enter** to Accept, **ESC** to Cancel

Using PRINTER
Press **P** to Change

Selecting **F4** will print the *current* record. You are given a second option, the **F6** key, that will allow you to print from the current record to the end. In fact, it usually allows you to print out approximately the next ten records.

To download, you may select either the **F4** or the **F6** key and this will retrieve the Print Entry screen shown above. You then need to select the **Press P to Change** option. Selecting this option will retrieve a screen that asks you to enter the printer or the name of the file for offline printing. Typing in the name of the file, its extension, and the letter of the drive that you intend to download to will allow you to download the records, for example,

A:Timor.doc

A is the disc drive letter, **Timor** is the meaningful name given to the file, and **doc** is the file's extension.

What you must remember is that the menu will not direct you to the download option, only to the print option, and it is through the print option that you are able to download the records to your disc.

Chapter 8

UMI Searching

UMI (University Microfilms International) is one of the more popular ondisc systems and many major databases are available through UMI. The main advantage of UMI is their well-developed searching software that offers both the beginner and the advanced searcher the opportunity to conduct effective searching. All the databases are supported by full-text services. You are able to obtain microform editions, photocopies, or bound copies of most of the works cited in their databases. UMI is the major international supplier of dissertations.

SOURCES OF INFORMATION

The following databases are a sample of what is available on UMI.

ABI/INFORM
Business Dateline Ondisc
Newspaper Abstracts Ondisc
Periodical Abstracts Ondisc
Resource/One Ondisc
Dissertation Abstracts Ondisc
INSPEC Ondisc

In this chapter you will learn the basics of UMI's searching protocol for two of the most popular databases that UMI supports: the ABI/INFORM database and Dissertation Abstracts ondisc.

The Databases in Detail

ABI/INFORM Ondisc

ABI/INFORM gives you access to current information in the following areas:

Accounting	Health Care	Law
Advertising	Human Resources	Marketing
Banking	Information Management	Real Estate
Data Processing	Insurance	Taxation
Financial Mgt	International Trade	Telecommunication

ABI/INFORM provides access to over 800 journals on business and management and indexes over 400 of those cover to cover. The records provided by ABI/INFORM provide concise abstracts of approximately 150 words that outline the contents of the journal articles.

Business Dateline Ondisc

Business Dateline Ondisc gives you access to current information in the following areas:

Mergers (acquisitions, expansions, and failures)
Business managers and executives
Products (New trends, marketing/production)
Business industries/conditions
Niche and specialty markets

Business Dateline ondisc provides access to over 180 regional business journals, newspapers, and business wire services. The database is extremely valuable because, in addition to full bibliographic details, it provides the complete text of the articles.

Newspaper Abstracts Ondisc

Newspaper Abstracts ondisc gives you access to articles from the major newspapers in the United States of America:

The Atlanta Constitution
The Boston Globe
The Chicago Tribune
The Christian Science Monitor
The Los Angeles Times
The Wall Street Journal
The Washington Post

Newspaper Abstracts ondisc provides abstracts of the articles it reviews, and all indexing is fully cross-referenced.

Periodical Abstracts Ondisc

Periodical Abstracts ondisc gives you access to information in the following areas:

Arts	Education
Business	Health
Commentary	Lifestyles
Computers	Literary Reviews
Consumer Issues	Politics
Current Events	Science

Periodical Abstracts ondisc provides access to over 450 journals in the above subject areas.

Resource/One Ondisc

Resource/One ondisc is a one-stop resource for information from both newspapers and journals. It gives an overview of topics ranging from computers to rock and roll taken from over 130 general interest journal articles. While the majority of the material is of a popular nature, users get full bibliographic details of the articles indexed as well as brief abstracts.

Dissertation Abstracts Ondisc

Dissertation Abstracts ondisc is one of the most valuable research products available ondisc. It provides information on doctoral dissertations and master's theses from 1861 to the present. The material after 1980 contains abstracts giving a brief outline of the study. The abstracts have the additional benefit of providing increased subject access since the abstract may be searched.

Dissertation Abstracts ondisc includes information from over 500 universities worldwide. The subject coverage is as wide as the research undertaken. The importance of this resource cannot be overstated.

INSPEC Ondisc

INSPEC ondisc gives you access to information in the following areas:

Computers and computer science
Electrical engineering
Electronics
Information technology
Physics

INSPEC ondisc indexes over 4,000 technical journals and over 1,000 conference proceedings in these subject areas.

SEARCHING ABI/INFORM ONDISC

UMI searching supports the types of search control that you have dealt with in the earlier chapters: Boolean searching, field-specific searching, and the use of truncation operators.

A record in ABI/INFORM will typically contain the following fields:

Title:
Authors:
Terms:
Codes:
Abstract:

Initial Menu

Below is the first menu that UMI's ABI/INFORM presents to you:

Main Menu

INTRODUCTION to ABI/INFORM
HOW TO USE ABI/INFORM Ondisc

SEARCH THE ABI/INFORM Database
CHANGE to another UMI disc
EXIT from System

To begin a search you need only tap the **ENTER** key since the search option is the default option on the initial menu. You will now be presented with the prompt *Search Term(s)*. At this point you are able to type in a term or combination of terms.

For this exercise you are interested in obtaining information on insider trading in the stock markets and whether it happens in Japan and Europe.

To start your search session, divide the search request into its basic concepts: insider trading (concept 1), stock markets (concept 2), Japan and Europe (concept 3). The next step is to determine how to relate these concepts in a manner that will allow you to answer your question. In this case, you will need to use the **AND** operator to link concept 1 (insider trading) and concept 2 (stock market). Concept 3 (Europe and Japan) consists of two parts, namely Europe and Japan. Therefore you will need to link the elements of concept 3 using the **OR** operator before you link concept 3 with concepts 1 and 2 using the **AND** operator, for example:

(INSIDER TRADING AND STOCK MARKET*) AND (EUROPE OR JAPAN)

The above search statement will retrieve the results you require. It is, however, a complex search statement incorporating the use of Boolean logic, brackets, and a truncation operator, the asterisk (*). As previously mentioned, it is always advisable to undertake your search *step by step* and break your search down into its component concepts:

Concept 1
Insider Trading retrieves 459 records

Concept 2
Stock Market retrieves 3635 records

Concept 3
Europe or Japan retrieves 19216 records

Searching for a phrase (two or more words) on UMI is very straightforward. You need only type in the terms in their natural order and UMI looks for those terms in that order. That is, in the above example, typing in the phrase **Insider Trading** after the search prompt would search on exactly what you type in and retrieve every occurrence of the words **Insider Trading** in that order. You are presented with the following screen on completion of the search:

Search terms		Item Count
(01):	insider –> INSIDER	938
(02):	trading –> TRADING	6306
(03):	(01) pre/1 (02)	459

Search results in 459 item(s)

If you examine the above illustration you will notice that each of the two terms were searched separately and later combined so that the term **INSIDER** preceded the term **TRADING** by 1 word [(01) pre/1 (02)]. Tapping the **F3** key (modify search) will return you to the search screen where you can now search on the other concepts. Note that on the search screen **insider trading** is shown as the first set. When you have finished searching on the remaining two concepts you will have a screen as shown below:

Previous Activities	**Item Count**
[1] insider trading	459
[2] stock market	3635
[3] japan or europe	19216

Search Term(s):

Now that you have established sets for each of the concepts that you wish to search, you will need to combine the sets. The procedure for using a set is to type in the numbers in the manner in which they occur on the screen. That is, you must type in the numbers within the [ ] (square brackets) as they appear on the screen. To combine the sets in the above example you need to type in the following at the search prompt:

[1] and [2] and [3]

The result set for the above search consists of eight records. To view the records, tap the **ENTER** key and you will be presented with the following title list:[1]

Title List

Item 1 of 8 in this Search

A Clockwork Future for Finanzplatz Schweiz?

Internationalization of Tokyo Stock Market

Cash-Rich Japanese Money Mangers Buy U.S. Theories

Squeezing the Manipulators: Japan Prepares to Tackle Insider Trading in . . .

Why Tokyo's Stock Market is Still Soaring After All These Years

Take a Second Look at the Second Section

Is Tokyo Really Quake Proof?

Global Exchanges: Markets Far and Wide

There are a number of useful advantages of the title list screen. First it allows you to quickly browse for suitable records. Second, it allows you to "Mark" the records for printing or downloading. Finally, it allows you to go to the record you are most interested in

---

1. Reprinted with permission from UMI.

directly, that is, by highlighting the title you wish to view and tapping the **ENTER** key you will retrieve the entire record. The color of the marked record will be different from the other records.

Below are three sample records from the result set [4].[2]

1 of 8

88-38827

Title: Squeezing the Manipulators: Japan Prepares to Tackle Insider Trading in Equities
Authors: Holloway, Nigel
Journal: Far Eastern Economic Review (Hong Kong) Vol: 141
Iss: 37 Date: Sep 15, 1988 pp: 92-93 Jrnl Code: FER ISSN: 0014-7591
Terms: Japan; Securities markets; Insider trading; Initial; Sales of securities (public); Legislation
Codes: 9170 (Non-US); 3400 (Investment analysis); 4320 (Legislation)
Abstract:
The increasing interrelation between stock markets around the world points to the need for harmonization of operations. This is especially evident in the case of Japan, whose shares total more than 40% of the value of all stocks traded worldwide. At a recent meeting in Stockholm, Sweden, US Securities & Exchange Commission Chairman David Ruder urged world stock market regulators to adopt industry-governing compatible legislation against such problems as market manipulation, insider trading, and misinformation. Market fraud is common in Japan, especially in the form of insider trading. For example, Japan's system, unlike that of the UK, permits underwriters of initial public offerings to allocate, rather than ration, shares. However, there are signs that the long-common practice of the privileged distribution of inside information may be changing.

---

2. Reprinted with permission from UMI.

86-32132
Title: Global Exchanges: Markets Far and Wide
Authors: Anonymous
Journal: Financial World Vol: 155 Iss: 19 Date: Sep 16, 1986 pp: 106-110 Jrnl Code: TWO ISSN: 0015-2064
Terms: International; Securities trading; Many countries; Stock exchanges (places); Trends
Codes: 9180 (International); 8130 (Investment services)
Abstract:
Globalization, or global trading, is inevitable because companies find it to be an efficient means of raising and shifting needed capital. In particular, investors are anxious to participate in the Japanese markets. However, Japan is not rushing to accommodate those investors. In contrast, the UK's London Stock Exchange is liberalizing its markets, aided by reforms that will become effective in October 1986. Some smaller foreign exchanges are hesitating to meet 2 of the international investors' preconditions: 1. liberalization of requirements to list, and 2. improvement of regulatory climates, whether by loosening or tightening rules. One specific challenge for US firms operating overseas will be establishing credibility on local terms. For example, insider trading, which is considered unfair in the US, is accepted in London and Tokyo. While several smaller European exchanges are expected to have trouble competing with the larger ones, Germany's stock market is considered one of the world's healthiest. Tables.

88-28934
Title: Why Tokyo's Stock Market Is Still Soaring After All These Years
Authors: Buell, Barbara; Holden, Ted; Glasgall, William
Journal: Business Week (Industrial/Technology Edition) Iss: 3062 Date: Jul 25, 1988 pp: 56-58 Jrnl Code: BWE ISSN: 0007-7135

Terms: Japan; Securities markets; Stock exchanges (places); Monetary policy; Securities trading; Insider trading
Codes: 9170 (Non-US); 8130 (Investment services)
Abstract:
Since its 1949 reopening, the Tokyo Stock Exchange's Nikkei Index has soared 16,000%, making the exchange the largest and best performing stock exchange in the world. On some days, volume on the Tokyo exchange exceeds 3-billion shares for its stocks, whose price-earnings ratios average 60, compared to the 14.5 ratio of the Standard & Poor's 500 on the New York Stock Exchange. Some say that the Tokyo stock market is rigged because the Japanese government uses the market and is able to direct it. Big brokers, banks, corporations, and bureaucrats from the Finance Ministry and the Bank of Japan have 3 primary goals in common: 1. a large personal savings rate, 2. high stock prices, and 3. low costs for raising capital. While the addition of foreign money into the exchange raises the possibility that the Japanese could lose some control over the market, analysts see little risk of a huge sell-off. The support given by the government to the market is illustrated by the Finance Ministry's change of accounting rules to prevent a sell-off of assets in March in order to declare trading losses in the wake of the October crash. Graphs.

Field-Specific Searching

In this section, Dissertation Abstracts ondisc will be used for the sample. It is essential that you become acquainted with field-specific searches since the fields are the key to effective searching. The procedure for field-specific searching in UMI is straightforward and may be readily used in conjunction with Boolean operators.

The following fields are searchable in Dissertation Abstracts ondisc:

Abstract
Author
Adviser
Date
School

Subject
Title

The procedure for field-specific searching is to use the field name, which is followed by the search term in brackets for example:

Author (Tevis, Walter)

or

Au (Tevis, Walter)

Searching for a particular Author or Title is very useful; however, it requires you to have some knowledge about the dissertation before you search. A more common situation is that you have a need for information about a particular subject. In this case you will need to conduct a subject search. The main subject field in DAI (Dissertation Abstracts International) is simply called Subject. The other fields that may be used in a subject search are the title and abstract fields. These fields must be used with discretion since the terms found in them may or may not reflect the subject of the dissertation. They are, however, still an important resource that may be used if searching the subject field is unsuccessful.

Subject Searching

For this example you are looking to see if anyone else has written a dissertation on the topic that you are thinking of researching: the perspective of education on violence in films. The three concepts from your query are violence (concept 1), film (concept 2), and education (concept 3).

The terms violence and *education* are suitable for use alone; the term *film*, however, should be linked to the term/phrase *motion picture* with the **OR** operator. Your search statement will appear as follows:

Violence AND Education AND (Film OR Motion Picture)

For this search, begin by searching on each of the concepts separately. Later, combine them when you have established a set for each concept. Remember that while you have several terms, the above search has only three concepts. Consider the following search results:

[1] Search: su (violence) 0
[2] Search: su (film or motion picture or television) 0
[3] Search: su (education) 3864

The above search is unsuccessful for the terms *violence* or *film/ motion picture/television*, as they are too specific for the subject field in DAI. The term education was successful, even with the limitation to the subject field, and 3,894 records were found. You will now need to repeat the first two searches and combine them with your third search on education. The following results were obtained when the same search was conducted without the field restrictions.

[4] Search: violence 94 item(s)
[5] Search: Search: film or motion picture 209 item(s)

The following result is achieved when sets [3], [4], and [5] are combined using the **AND** operator:

[6] Search: [3] and [4] and [5] 1 item(s)

While the above search only retrieved a single record, it must be noted that the search has been conducted using the January 1991-June 1991 Humanities ondisc database. To get significant results, a search of the whole database would be carried out.

The following record was retrieved from the above search set.[3] Locate each of the terms searched. Review the record and make note of the fields in which the search terms are located.

Author: DEL COLLE, PAUL LAWRENCE
Title: THE EYE OF THE BEHOLDER: THE SOCIAL AND CULTURAL SIGNIFICANCE OF TELEVISION AS REFLECTED IN THE WORK OF TELEVISION RE- PORTERS AND CRITICS FOR SELECTED U.S.

---

3. Reprinted with permission from UMI.

NEWSPAPERS, 1976–1986 (SOCIAL SIGNIFICANCE, UNITED STATES)
School: NEW YORK UNIVERSITY (0146) Degree: PHD Date: 1990 pp: 235
Adviser: POSTMAN, NEIL
Source: DAI 51/08A, p. 2554
Pub. No.: AAC9102611
Subject: JOURNALISM (0391); MASS COMMUNICATIONS (0708); EDUCATION, SOCIAL SCIENCES (0534)

Abstract:

Theorist Neil Postman has proposed that schools should adopt a curriculum of media education, dubbed "media ecology," in order to monitor–and thereby regulate–the deleterious effects of television on society. Since schools and news media seem to serve similar, educative functions, it was proposed that newspapers could also monitor television's impact. Thus, a study was undertaken to determine whether reporters and critics who cover television for selected newspapers have conveyed a sense of television's social and cultural significance. The writings of five television scholars were previewed. These works were distilled into corresponding arguments, or "premises," against which the content of newspapers could be compared. The five authors and their respective premises were Marshall McLuhan (subversion of logic), Neil Postman (television as a learning system), George Gerbner (violence), Rose Goldsen (desensitization), and Todd Gitlin (hegemony). *The New York Times, The Washington Post,* and *The Los Angeles Times* were chosen for the study. The so-called "Arts and Culture" sections which appeared in the Sunday editions of these newspapers were surveyed for news coverage and commentary about television. The years 1976, 1978, 1980, 1982, 1984, and 1986 were sampled. References to the premises listed above were recorded by citing specific words or passages in the newspaper columns. The contexts of the commentaries and columns were also considered. Slightly fewer than three thousand columns were included in the survey. It was concluded that reporters and critics in newspapers have generally made some efforts to convey a sense of television's social and cultural impact. However, these efforts have not been sufficient to truly provide the public with a general awareness of the issues which surround the medium. Substantive criticism of television seemed to decline, or "soften," after 1980. A concern was voiced that, while each newspaper mentioned each scholarly premise at least once, there were virtually no references to the scholars themselves as the originators of these theories regarding television's impact. It was recommended that newspapers should behave more like schools. That is, certain columns on television's impact should be offered regularly, just as schools offer classes. Some formal training in television theory should be required of journalists as well. It was also recommended that newspapers and universities should institute exchange programs, with scholars temporarily trading places with journalists. Thus, the culture of the classroom could infiltrate the culture of the newsroom. Hopefully, a more socially responsible journalism would result.

This record clearly indicates that the abstract is a substantial part of the record in Dissertation Abstracts. The value of abstracts must never be underestimated. The importance of the abstract as a form of subject access is increased in the above example by the broad or general nature of the terms found in the subject field.

DOWNLOADING

The procedure for downloading the records that you have retrieved from your search begins from either the title screen or the screen that displays the full record. Using the title screen is the most efficient approach. It is advisable to "mark" the record that you intend to download.

To mark a record you must tap the **SPACE BAR** while the title is highlighted. A small arrowhead will appear to the left of the title to indicate that the record is highlighted. When you display a highlighted record you will see that the color of the record is different from the other records. To unmark, you must again tap the **SPACE BAR** while your cursor is on the record that you wish to unmark. It is alway easier to mark the records that you are interested in so that they can be identified when you start the procedure for downloading.

The procedure for downloading can commence either at the title list screen or the screen that displays the full record. First, you must tap the **F4** (output) key. After tapping the **F4** key, you will be presented with the following menu:

Output Options

Format: Long (Citation and abstract)
    Short (Citation only)
Output to: Printer only

    Printer and disk file
    Disk file only

Drive: B:

Filename: \UMI.TXT

To select your option you must highlight the desired option and tap the **ENTER** key. This will bring you to the following menu:

What do you want to Output?

Marked Items

Current Item

All items (Max= 10)

To choose your selection you must again highlight the desired option and tap the **ENTER** key. While the third option suggests that the maximum number of items that you may download is ten, there is in fact no limit if you have marked the records that you intend to download. Selecting the Marked Items option allows you to download all the records you have marked.

Chapter 9

Compact Cambridge Searching

Compact Cambridge is a comprehensive ondisc vendor in the health and biological sciences, and offers databases in a wide variety of subject areas.

In this chapter you will learn the basics of Compact Cambridge's searching protocol on one of the most popular databases that Compact Cambridge supports, the Health database. Compact Cambridge is a popular ondisc system and many of the major databases are available through Compact Cambridge. The main advantage of Compact Cambridge is its well-developed searching software that offers full Boolean search logic and field-specific searching. It also allows you to search in two distinct forms, a **MENU** mode for the beginner and a **COMMAND** mode for the experienced searcher.

Searching on Compact Cambridge ondisc is very powerful and precise in that all fields may be searched and searches can be restricted to any field or groups of fields. When phrases are searched, the phrases must be placed within quotation marks.

SOURCES OF INFORMATION

The following databases are a sample of what is available on Compact Cambridge CD ROM.

ASEA CD
CANCERLIT (Cancer Literature)
DRUG INFORMATION CENTER CD
LIFE SCIENCES COLLECTION CD
MEDLINE CD
PDQ (Physicians' Data Query) CD

HEALTH DATABASE

Health–Planning and Administration

Compact Cambridge searching supports the types of search control that we have dealt with in the earlier chapters: Boolean searching, field-specific searching, and the use of truncation operators.

The Health database covers over ten years of health information on the nonclinical aspects of health delivery. The database is compiled by the National Library of Medicine (USA) and is distributed from the NLM by Cambridge Scientific Abstracts. The subject coverage includes planning and administration of health facilities, health insurance, personnel administration and quality assurance.

SEARCHING THE HEALTH DATABASE

A record in the Health database ondisc will typically contain the following fields:

: SJ	:	SUBJECT [TI, MJ, MN, MW, AB]
: MM	:	MAJOR/MINOR SUBJECT HEADINGS [MJ, MN]
: *	:	ALL
: UI	:	UNIQUE IDENTIFIER
: AU	:	AUTHOR
: AF	:	AUTHOR AFFILIATION
: TI	:	TITLE
: SO	:	SOURCE
: PY	:	PUBLICATION YEAR
: LA	:	LANGUAGE
: MJ	:	MAJOR SUBJECT HEADING
: MN	:	MINOR SUBJECT HEADING
: PS	:	PERSONAL NAME AS SUBJECT
: AB	:	ABSTRACT
: PT	:	PUBLICATION TYPE
: IS	:	ISSN
: ID	:	ID NUMBER
: LI	:	SPECIAL LIST INDICATOR

: SB : JOURNAL SUBSET
: SI : SECONDARY SOURCE ID
: JC : JOURNAL CODE
: EM : ENTRY MONTH
: NM : NEW MATERIAL

Initial Menu

Below is the first menu that Compact Cambridge presents to you. First, you are given the choice of two searching modes, the **Menus** mode and the **Commands** mode. The **Menus** mode is suitable for the beginning searcher and will assist you in carrying out your search. The **Commands** mode is available for the experienced searcher and allows you to enter the commands directly at the dot prompt. Below is an illustration of the initial menu.

Select Function

Menus
Commands
Change Compact Disc
CC configuration
Dos commands
What's New
eXit

Menu Searching on Compact Cambridge

To begin your search session, highlight **Menus** using your arrow key and then tap the **Enter** key once. You are now presented with the following menu options:

Limit Expand MeSH Search Display Print Keep Format Macro Clr.

For this exercise you are interested in the relationship between fitness and sport to see if you can become fit without having to do conventional exercises.

Before you begin your search you will need to break the search request down into its basic concepts: fitness, sport, and exercise. The next step is to determine how to relate these concepts in a manner that will enable you to achieve an answer to your question. In this case, you will need to use the **AND** operator to link concept 1 (fitness) and concept 2 (sport), and to use the **NOT** operator to exclude concept 3 (exercise).

It is wise to conduct your searches separately and do your logical connections later. This allows you to see the number of records retrieved (hits) for each part of your search. To begin the actual search, highlight the **Menus** option and tap the **ENTER** key. You will now be presented with a menu asking you to type in your search term. Type in the term *fitness* and tap the **ENTER** key. You will then be presented with the menu that allows you to select the field you wish to search. In this case, choose the **All** option by highlighting it and tapping the **Enter** key. You are now presented with the menu that asks you to select the operator (connector) with which to link the terms. In this case, since you have only entered a single term, select the first option, **NONE**, by highlighting it and tap the **ENTER** key once. Then repeat the same procedure for the terms *Sport* and *Excerises*. You should achieve the following result:

Set No.	Search terms	No. of Records
# 1	Fitness	2199
# 2	Sport	215
# 3	Exercises	3289

To answer your question, you must use the Boolean operators to logically link the above sets (concepts). Compact Cambridge software will allow you to combine the sets in the following manner:

1. Select the **SELECT** command and tap the **ENTER** key
2. Type in your set numbers (e.g., #1 **AND** #2 **ANDNOT** #3)

Note, in the above example, that **ANDNOT** was used to achieve the function of the **NOT** operator. This does not in any way affect the search logic. It is just the protocol used by Compact Cambridge to express the **NOT** function.

The above combination will give you the following result:

Set No.	Search terms	No. of Records
#1	Fitness	2199
#2	Sport	215
#3	Exercises	3289
#4	Fitness AND Sport ANDNOT Exercises	43

At this point, since you have a result set, Set #4 with 43 records, you can either accept this result set or take the opportunity to refine your search request further. For example, if, on further consideration, you realize that you are primarily concerned with sport and fitness in teenagers, you can refine the search as follows:

Concept #5 = teenager

You will now need to think of alternative or analogous terms to enable you to maximize your retrieval with the **OR** operator before you refine your search with the **AND** operator.

Concept #5 = teenager* OR youth* OR adolescence*

The above three terms can now be put in a single search request by placing the **OR** operator between each term. To begin the actual search, highlight the command menu option **SEARCH** and tap the **ENTER** key once. You will now be presented with a menu asking you to type in your search terms. After you type in the three terms, **teenager* or youth* or adolescence***, tap the **ENTER** key once and you will be presented with a menu asking you to select the fields that you wish to search. Use the arrow key to highlight the **ALL** option and tap the **ENTER** key once. Your search will be conducted on each of the terms separately and then combined. Your search should achieve the following results (note the truncation operator, *, was used at the end of each term, e.g., **teenager*** to increase the recall):

Set No.	Search terms	No. of Records
#5	Teenager*	426
#6	Youth*	775
#7	Adolescence*	30,221
#8	Teenager* OR Youth* OR adolescence*	30,433

In the above example you can see that by using the **OR** operator between the terms, you retrieved more records in the combination set (#8) than in any of the sets with only a single term (#5,#6,#7).

You will now need to combine concept 8 (**teenager* OR youth* OR adolescence***) with your first result set. To begin the actual search, highlight the menu option **Search** and tap the **ENTER** key. You will now be presented with a menu asking you to type in your search terms. Type in Set numbers #4 and #8. You should obtain the following results:

Set No.	Search terms	No. of Records
#9	(Sport AND Fitness) AND (Teenager* OR Youth* OR Adolescence*) ANDNOT Exercises	18

The following two records are examples of records from the result Set #9:[1]

Output generated from Compact Cambridge: HEALTH

Search Strategy:

((SPORT[ALL]) AND (FITNESS[ALL]) ANDNOT (EXERCISES[ALL])) AND (TEENAGER*[ALL] OR YOUTH*[ALL] OR ADOLESCENCE*[ALL])

---

1. Reprinted with permission from Compact Cambridge.

DOCUMENT 1 of 2:

UI: UNIQUE IDENTIFIER
88270564
AU: AUTHOR
Kibler WB; McQueen C; Uhl T
AF: AUTHOR AFFILIATION
Sports Medicine Center, Lexington, Kentucky.
TI: TITLE
Fitness evaluations and fitness findings in competitive junior tennis players.
SO: SOURCE
CLIN-SPORTS-MED; 1988 Apr; 7(2); P 403-16
PY: PUBLICATION YEAR
1988
LA: LANGUAGE
English
MJ: MAJOR SUBJECT HEADING
Athletic Injuries:PP. Competitive Behavior:. Physical Fitness:. Repetition Strain Injury:PP. Sports:. Tennis:
MN: MINOR SUBJECT HEADING
Adolescence:. Adult:. Child:. Female:. Human:. Male:. Muscles:PP. Physical Education and Training:MT
AB: ABSTRACT

Elite tennis players, as well as a large number of active recreational players, are involved in a sport that applies high repetitive loads that can create tension overload situations in certain key anatomic areas of the body and add to possible overload situations in other areas of the body. This results in patterns of inflexibility and weakness that can be demonstrated on a tennis-specific musculoskeletal exam, and that can be correlated with areas of increased injury occurrence. These players report conditioning programs that are, for the most part, inadequate to confer total conditioning of all the muscular parameters important in playing tennis. All of these factors, in addition to the frequency and type of playing, contribute to the occurrence of the overload injuries noted. These aspects need to be addressed in a preventative program for injury reduction. We do

not believe that major changes in the way that tennis is played should be implemented until the effects of a proper preventative conditioning program are evaluated. The "ideal" conditioning program has not yet been found. While the exact composition of the program is in doubt, our studies allow us to recommend flexibility, strength, and endurance training for all athletes playing tennis at frequent intervals. This program should be guided by the findings on the preparticipation exam. ABSTRACT.
PT: PUBLICATION TYPE
REVIEW; REVIEW, TUTORIAL
IS: ISSN
0278-5919
RF: NUMBER OF REFERENCES
18
SB: JOURNAL SUBSET
M; MEDLINE-PRIORITY-JOURNAL
SI: SECONDARY SOURCE ID
MED/88270564
JC: JOURNAL CODE
CSM
EM: ENTRY MONTH
8810

DOCUMENT 2 of 2:

UI: UNIQUE IDENTIFIER
86091460
AU: AUTHOR
Berg KE; LaVoie JC; Latin RW
TI: TITLE
Physiological training effects of playing youth soccer.
SO: SOURCE
MED-SCI-SPORTS-EXERC; 1985 Dec; 17(6); P 656-60
PY: PUBLICATION YEAR
1985
LA: LANGUAGE
English

MJ: MAJOR SUBJECT HEADING
Physical Education and Training:. Physical Fitness:. Soccer:. Sports:
MN: MINOR SUBJECT HEADING
Biomechanics:. Body Height:. Body Weight:. Child:. Heart Rate:. Human:. Knee Joint:PH. Male:. Oxygen Consumption:. Pulmonary Gas Exchange:. Total Lung Capacity:
AB: ABSTRACT
> The purpose of this investigation was to determine if a 9-wk youth soccer program had any effect on cardiorespiratory fitness (VO2max and VO2submax), peak knee torque, and flexibility. Subjects were 20 sixth grade boys, 11 of whom were members of a YMCA soccer team: 9 were normally active boys who were not participating in any organized sport during the study who served as a control group. Mean ages (+/− SD) were 11.8 +/− 0.34 and 11.5 +/− 0.60 yr for the soccer and control group, respectively. Initial VO2max values of 49.83 and 47.42 ml . kg − 1 . min − 1 for the soccer and the control group, respectively, are similar to those reported in the literature for untrained normal boys of this age. Results indicated that playing soccer three times weekly increased VEmax and reduced VO2 (ml . kg − 1 . min − 1 and 1 . min − 1) at a submaximal running speed (all P's less than 0.05), while no change in VO2max was noted. No significant training effect was observed in peak knee torque or flexibility subsequent to soccer training. It is concluded that the effects of playing soccer in these subjects resulted in no change in cardiorespiratory fitness, peak knee torque, or flexibility. ABSTRACT.

IS: ISSN
0195-9131
SB: JOURNAL SUBSET
M; MEDLINE-PRIORITY-JOURNAL
SI: SECONDARY SOURCE ID
MED/86091460
JC: JOURNAL CODE
MG8
EM: ENTRY MONTH
8604

Command Searching on Compact Cambridge

To begin a command search you will need to select the **Commands** option from the **Select Function** menu by highlighting it and tapping the **ENTER** key once. The **Commands** screen has a dot prompt and a menu as shown below:

Limit Expand MEsh Search Display Print Keep
Table Options eXit

The following commands are available in the command mode:

C	(Clear) clears the screen, tables and limits.
D	(Display) displays records from Result Sets.
DOS	(DOS) allows you to execute DOS commands.
E	(Expand) allows access to the index of terms.
F	(Format) allows you to change the record format.
O	(Options) offers you a list of commands.
L	(Limit) offers a prescribed list of limit options.
M	(Macro) allows you to create or list Macros.
MD	(Macro Drive) allows you to seek Macros in another drive.
ME	(MeSH) displays MeSH subject terms/phrases.
P	(Print) presents you with the print options.
S	(Search) allows you to search the database.
T	(Table) displays the result sets.
X	(Exit) allows you to exit the program.

For this example, you are looking for information on birth control for men. You will need to identify the concepts in your search question before starting the search. Two concepts can be clearly identified: concept 1 (birth control) and concept 2 (men). Your first concept, birth control, is a phrase rather than a single term and you will need to pay special attention to the searching protocol. The procedure for searching on phrases is software-specific. Compact Cambridge requires that you use quotation marks on both sides of a phrase. For example, **"birth control"** will retrieve all occurrences of the term **Birth** adjacent to the term **Control**. You can also choose to search on terms that are separated by a number of words. For example, **birth w3 control** will retrieve all occurrences of the term *birth* within three words of the term *control*. For your purpose here, simply searching for **"Birth Control"** as a phrase, using the quotation marks, is the most suitable choice.

To begin the actual search in the command mode, you need to type **S** at the dot prompt. For example, searching by typing in **.S "Birth Control"** will retrieve the following:

Set No.	Search terms	No. of Records
#1	"Birth Control" [ALL]	150

The above is the first step toward answering your question. You now have concept 1 (birth control) in a form that you can combine with concept 2 (men). For example, searching on the result set #1 with the term *men* by typing **S #1 AND men** will retrieve the following:

Set No.	Search Terms	No. of Records
#2	("Birth Control"[ALL] AND Men [ALL]	10

The following two records are examples of records from the result set #2:[2]

Output generated from Compact Cambridge: HEALTH

---

2. Reprinted with permission from Compact Cambridge.

DOCUMENT 1 of 2:

UI: UNIQUE IDENTIFIER
89227587
AU: AUTHOR
McCormick NB; Gaeddert W
AF: AUTHOR AFFILIATION
Department of Psychology, State University of New York College, Plattsburgh 12901.
TI: TITLE
Power in college students' contraceptive decisions.
SO: SOURCE
ARCH-SEX-BEHA^; 1989 Feb; 18(1); P 35-48
PY: PUBLICATION YEAR
1989
LA: LANGUAGE
English
MJ: MAJOR SUBJECT HEADING
Decision Making:. Family Planning:. Knowledge, Attitudes, Practice:. Power (Psychology):
MN: MINOR SUBJECT HEADING
Adolescence:. Adult:. Female:. Gender Identity:. Human:. Male:. Pilot Projects:. Stereotyping:
AB: ABSTRACT
>Excluding Hollerbach (1980), previous fertility researchers have paid little attention to contraceptive power bases, relationships that become the source of changes in birth control values and behavior. Eight contraceptive power bases, each evaluated as a direct or obvious strategy, were identified in a pilot study involving 25 college students as participants and 10 undergraduate raters. Two-hundred college students completed a questionnaire which included the Bem Sex Role Inventory, inquired into their sexual and contraceptive behavior, and asked about contraceptive power bases. There were highly significant main effects for both students' personal experiences with contraceptive power bases and for their opinions about the comfort and effectiveness of same. Coercion was the most popular and legitimate power was the least popular power

base. Women were more likely than men to be the targets of contraceptive power bases, the majority of which were stereotyped as feminine by women in particular. Sex role identification was unrelated to students' experiences with contraceptive power bases. The implications of these findings for family-planning researchers and practitioners are addressed. ABSTRACT.
IS: ISSN
0004-0002
SB: JOURNAL SUBSET
M; MEDLINE-PRIORITY-JOURNAL
SI: SECONDARY SOURCE ID
MED/89227587
JC: JOURNAL CODE
8GR
EM: ENTRY MONTH
8908

DOCUMENT 2 of 2:

UI: UNIQUE IDENTIFIER
84091566
AU: AUTHOR
Finkel ML; Finkel DJ
TI: TITLE
Male adolescent sexual behavior, the forgotten partner: a review.
SO: SOURCE
J-SCH-HEALTH; 1983 Nov; 53(9); P 544-7
PY: PUBLICATION YEAR
1983
LA: LANGUAGE
English
MJ: MAJOR SUBJECT HEADING
Sex Behavior:
MN: MINOR SUBJECT HEADING
Adolescence:. Contraception Behavior:. Human:. Knowledge, Attitudes, Practice:. Male:. Psychosexual Development:. Sex Maturation:

AB: ABSTRACT
It is encouraging that after years of focusing attention on the female's ability and responsibility to manage her reproductive behavior, the male is finally beginning to receive notice and attention. Ironically, before the widespread use of the Pill and the IUD, men and male birth control methods played an important role in family planning. Even today, reliance on vasectomies, the condom and withdrawal account for 25% of the contraceptive use among couples and trend statistics point to an increased interest among selected populations in the use of barrier methods that require partner cooperation for effective use. Yet, most small scale and nationwide knowledge, attitudes and practice (KAP) studies focus on the female, particularly the teen-age female. With the exception of fragmentary survey data, pertinent information about male adolescent sexual activity is virtually nonexistent. The growing consensus among researchers and planners is that it is now crucial to research the forgotten partner–the adolescent male. ABSTRACT.

IS: ISSN
0022-4391
SB: JOURNAL SUBSET
M; MEDLINE-PRIORITY-JOURNAL; N; NURSING-SUBSET
SI: SECONDARY SOURCE ID
MED/84091566
JC: JOURNAL CODE
K13
EM: ENTRY MONTH
8404

Field-Specific Searching

In the following example your search request is on traditional medicine in the countries of India, China, and Japan. You will again need to break the search down into its concepts. The first concept is traditional medicine (concept 1). The second concept is the geographical location.

As concept 1, traditional medicine *is* a two-word phrase. You could place the quotation marks on either side of the terms to retrieve them together. However, in this case, using the adjacency operator within (**w1**) between the two terms (i.e., **traditional w1 medicine**) will be more suitable. It will allow you to retrieve traditional Chinese medicine or traditional Japanese medicine, etc. With concept 2, geographical location, you will need to connect the relevant countries with the **OR** operator (i.e., **India OR China OR Japan**).

To begin, start your search by typing in **S** at the dot prompt (Command mode), followed by the terms **traditional w1 medicine**. You should receive the following results:

Set. No.	Search terms	No. of Records
#1	Traditional	2707
#2	Medicine	31809
#3	Traditional w1 Medicine	108

In the above illustration, the result set #3 gives you all the records containing the terms *traditional* and *medicine* within one word of each other. For example, the phrase traditional native medicine or traditional Chinese medicine would both be retrieved in the results of set #3. The next step is to start another search on concept 2.

Concept 2 requires the use of the **OR** operator to link the countries of China, India, and Japan together. You will also need to use a field-specific operator to limit your search to the Minor descriptor field (MN). The reason for using the Minor descriptor restriction, rather than the Major descriptor restriction, is that countries and place names are typically put in the Minor descriptor field, while the Major descriptor field is reserved for subject headings. Using the field restriction of the Minor descriptor field will enable you to limit your search to only those articles that include the designated countries as a significant aspect of the record.

This search should achieve the following results:

Set No.	Search terms	No. of Records
#4	India[MN]	1942
#5	China[MN]	696
#6	Japan[MN]	1347
#7	India[MN] OR China[MN] OR Japan[MN]	3912

To finish your search you will need to combine the two result sets
with the **AND** operator (i.e., sets #3 and #7). This should give you
the following result:

Set No.	Search terms	No. of Records
#8	((Traditional w1 Medicine) AND (India[MN] OR China [MN] OR Japan[MN])).	13

The following two records are examples of records from the
result set #8:[3]

Output generated from Compact Cambridge:
HEALTH 1982–May 1991

Search Strategy:

**((JAPAN[MN] OR CHINA[MN] OR INDIA[MN])) AND
(TRADITIONAL[ALL] W1 MEDICINE[ALL])**

DOCUMENT 1 of 2:

UI: UNIQUE IDENTIFIER
88057959
AU: AUTHOR
Chen HH
TI: TITLE
Integrating ancient and modern medicine in Chinese hospitals. The
interaction among technology, traditional Chinese medicine, and
health care.
SO: SOURCE
INT-J-TECHNOL-ASSESS-HEALTH-CARE; 1987; 3(2); P 265-73
PY: PUBLICATION YEAR
1987

---

3. Reprinted with permission from Compact Cambridge.

LA: LANGUAGE
English
MJ: MAJOR SUBJECT HEADING
Hospitals:. Medicine, Chinese Traditional:. Sociology, Medical:. Technology, Medical:TD
MN: MINOR SUBJECT HEADING
China:. Interinstitutional Relations:
AB: ABSTRACT
> Modern industrial society and its industrial processes can sometimes discourage the practice of traditional medicine. The existence and use of traditional Chinese medicine for several thousands of years indicates that it has sound elements. As has been true with features of other ancient, highly developed civilizations, the discipline of traditional Chinese medicine offers a valuable resource in the treatment and prevention of disease. Its scientific aspects and valuable experiences must continue to be developed according to Western scientific methodology. China has initiated a program to utilize modern industrialized technology in the integration of the traditional Chinese and modern Western medical systems. The policy and process aimed at integrating traditional Chinese medicine with Western medicine are presented in this paper. These measures have resulted in considerable utilization and development of the traditional Chinese medicine system, and have had a major impact on the development of public health care, as well as medical technology and science. The positive interactions between these fields of study and existing problems are discussed, and some comments on future expectations are presented. ABSTRACT.

IS: ISSN
0266-4623
LI: SPECIAL LIST INDICATOR
HEALTH-FILE
SI: SECONDARY SOURCE ID
AHA/88057959
JC: JOURNAL CODE
GTI
EM: ENTRY MONTH
8803

DOCUMENT 2 of 2:

UI: UNIQUE IDENTIFIER
83171587
AU: AUTHOR
Ramachandran H; Shastri GS
TI: TITLE
Movement for medical treatment. A study in contact patterns of a rural population.
SO: SOURCE
SOC-SCI-MED; 1983; 17(3); P 177-87
PY: PUBLICATION YEAR
1983
LA: LANGUAGE
English
MJ: MAJOR SUBJECT HEADING
Health Services Accessibility:ST. Rural Health:
MN: MINOR SUBJECT HEADING
Attitude to Health:. Catchment Area (Health):. Communication:. Human:. India:. Medicine, Traditional:. Patient Acceptance of Health Care:. Socioeconomic Factors:
AB: ABSTRACT

This paper deals with the patterns of movement of rural population for purposes of medical treatment. The following hypothesis are empirically tested with the data on 245 randomly selected sample villages containing about 30,000 households in Tumkur District of Karnataka (India). (a) There are significant differences in the incidence of sickness between various socio-economic groups. (b) The poorer sections of the rural society tend to get treated by informal/traditional systems of medicine. (c) Since the available medical facilities are few, no significant differences are observable in the distance travelled by different socio-economic groups. (d) The actual places of visit for treatment may be different for different socio-economic groups, since the society consists of 'status-conscious' population. (e) The long distance movement is not a matter of travel costs but essentially of overhead costs at the places of treatment. The analysis reveals that hypothesis (c), (d) and (e) are valid. Inval-

idation of hypothesis (a) raises the question of perception of sickness among the various strata of the society, whereas invalidation of hypothesis (b) indicates the use of allopathic system by all sections of rural population. In terms of location planning of medical services, the study indicates that two levels may be thought of–neighbourhood facilities and higher order facilities– rather than a hierarchy of medical centres involving a number of intermediary levels. Middle level centres are found to be underutilised since the patients tend to bypass them to avail of medical services of higher order centres. ABSTRACT.
IS: ISSN
0277-9536
SB: JOURNAL SUBSET
M; MEDLINE-PRIORITY-JOURNAL
SI: SECONDARY SOURCE ID
MED/83171587
JC: JOURNAL CODE
UT9
EM: ENTRY MONTH
8307

DOWNLOADING

Downloading allows you to store the results from a search in a file on your floppy disc. To download your results with Compact Cambridge ondisc, you can use the following steps:

1. First, Select the **Keep** option from the menu by highlighting it with the arrow key and tapping the **ENTER** key once.
2. You will be presented with a screen that offers the last set created as the default option. You are able to accept the default option or identify the set number you wish to download (#9).
3. You are now presented with a screen that allows you to name the file for the documents. This step also requires that you identify the disc drive to which you intend to send the records (e.g., **B:test.doc** where **B:** indicates the drive, **test** is the filename, and **doc** is the extension). Note there must always be a period between the filename and its extension.

Chapter 10
AUSTROM Searching

AUSTROM is the Australian social science and education databases on CD ROM.

SOURCES OF INFORMATION

The AUSTROM CD ROM contains thirteen Australian databases in the social sciences and education.

AEI	Australian Education Index
APAIS	Australian Public Affairs Information Service
ARCH	Australian Architecture Database
ASCIS (CRA)	Australian Schools Catalog Information Service (Curriculum Resources Abstracts)
AUSPORT	
CINCH	Australian Criminology Database
EDLINE	
FAMILY	Australian Family and Society Abstracts
HEI	Home Economics Index
LEISURE	
PINPOINTER	Australian Index to Leisure Activities and Consumer Reports
WESTDOC	

There is also a Journal Index file that shows which journals are indexed by which database.

The Databases in Detail

Australian Education Index (AEI)

AEI contains over 45,000 records on topics such as educational policy, research, administration, psychology, sociology, and library and information science. The source documents are both published and unpublished including journal articles, monographs, research reports, theses, conference papers, parliamentary debates, legislation, and newspaper articles.

Australian Public Affairs Information Service (APAIS)

APAIS contains over 158,000 records on Australian political, legal, economic, and social matters. APAIS provides subject access to current information from newspaper articles, scholarly journals, conference papers, and books in the social sciences and humanities.

The Australian Architecture Database (ARCH)

ARCH contains over 8,000 records on material related to architecture and building information in Australia and New Zealand.

Australian Schools Catalogue Information Service (Curriculum Resources Abstracts) (ASCIS–CRA)

ASCIS (CRA) contains over 7,000 records relating to primary and post-primary education in Australia.

AUSPORT

AUSPORT contains over 4,000 references on Australian sports- and leisure-related topics.

Australian Criminology Database (CINCH)

CINCH contains over 20,000 records on material related to criminology in Australia. The material covered is taken from journal articles, book reviews, monographs, conference papers, theses, government documents, statistical publications, and unpublished sources.

EDLINE

EDLINE contains over 5,000 bibliographic records on material related to curriculum, educational management, educational psychology, educational sociology, schools, and teaching. The material covered is taken from books, journal articles, reports, policy documents, and pamphlets.

Australian Family and Society Abstracts (FAMILY)

FAMILY contains over 13,000 records on legal, sociological, psychological, demographic, and economic issues. The material covered is taken from books, journal articles, conference papers, government reports, discussion papers, statistical documents, annual reports, bibliographies, and theses.

Home Economics Index (HEI)

HEI contains over 1,700 records on material concerned with home economics. The HEI is a subject index to periodical literature and only covers periodical literature published in 1989.

LEISURE

LEISURE contains over 22,000 records concerned with sport, recreation, and tourism in Australia.

Australian Index to Leisure Activities and Consumer Reports (PINPointer)

PINPOINTER provides a subject index to popular and practical material published in periodical literature in Australia. It contains over 13,000 records.

WESTDOC

WESTDOC contains over 9,000 records of material that relates to the Western Region of Melbourne.

SEARCHING AUSTROM–OVERVIEW

To begin a search with AUSTROM you must start by selecting one of the thirteen databases available on the AUSTROM disc. The details of the various databases are given in the previous section. For this example you will begin by selecting the database APAIS. APAIS stands for Australian Public Affairs and Information Service.

There are three basic steps to start searching:

1. Select the field that you wish to search.
2. Select and enter the word/phrase that you wish to search on.
3. Display the set that was created as a result of your search.

Having selected APAIS, you will need to start your search by selecting the field or the part of the record that you wish to search initially. To present the field options you will need to press the **F3** function key. You will be given a choice among the following fields:

Title
Author
Source
Input Date
Descriptors–by phrase
Descriptors–by keyword
Identifiers
Cross search
Notes
User Added field 1
User Added field 2

The title field gives a rough form of subject access in that titles invariably contain terms relevant to the subject at hand. However, the "subject" terms found in the title may not be consistent from one article to the next and may not properly represent the subject of the article. Thus, subject access via the title field should be used with caution.

Titles are, of course, part of the formal citation of a record, and title information will be given in all instances where an article is referred to or cited. Accordingly, they are an important means of access to a record.

The author field will contain the article's author, whether the author is a personal author or a corporate author. Finding a record via a corporate author can retrieve a host of material on relevant topics. For example, requesting material for which the Department of Mines is the author would invariably retrieve material on mining. Requesting material for which Greenpeace is the corporate author would invariably retrieve material on environmental issues.

The descriptors and identifiers fields are the key to subject searching. Selection of the descriptors field will uncover the majority of records for a particular subject term. The key to effective use of the descriptors field lies in the use of the printed APAIS thesaurus.

The descriptors field is the formal subject approach field and all terms/phrases found in the descriptors field will be found in the APAIS thesaurus. The identifiers field is used for new or marginal subject terms or place names that are not yet contained in APAIS thesaurus.

The thesaurus will give you the precise terms used in the descriptors and, more importantly, tell you the other terms they represent. The following is an excerpt from the APAIS Thesaurus:

*Taxation Jan 78
- **UF** Duties
  Indirect taxation

- **BUF** Consumption tax
  Death duties
  Excise duties

- **NT** Company tax
  Fringe benefits tax
  Income tax
  Land tax
  Payroll tax
  Rates (Property)
  Sales tax
  Stamp duties
  Value added tax

- **RT** Economic policy
  Finance, Public
  Licences
  Tariffs
  Tax avoidance
  Tax reform

The identifiers field is used for new or marginal terms. The identifiers field is of particular value in APAIS since the database is a topical one and new terms are constantly being introduced.

The abstract field will give you a precis or summary of the record's content. The value of the abstract field must not be overlooked. It is important in that it provides you with a concise review of the article and states the pertinent elements of the article. The abstract field may also be used as a rough form of subject access to the contents of the article. Just as with the title field, the use of the abstract field for subject access must be done with caution since some of the terms contained within the abstract will not reflect the record's content and even the relevant terms may not be used consistently from record to record.

The Cross search option is the one that allows you to search *across* all the searchable fields in the record. It is a useful searching procedure for finding uncommon terms or hard-to-locate information.

SEARCHING APAIS ON AUSTROM

To begin this example, assume that you need information on foreign relations between the United States and Australia in the year 1990.

First, you must select the concepts that appear in the search question *before* you begin your search. Three main concepts of the above search are foreign relations, United States, and Australia. The fourth concept, 1990, will be used as an option later.

If you examine the three concepts in the above question, you will notice that each of the concepts is required in your proposed result. This means that you will eventually need to connect the concepts with the **AND** operator.

To begin the actual search, you must select a field from the list of available fields to search. Select the most commonly used subject access field, the descriptor field. You choose the field by "going" to it with the arrow keys and then placing the cursor on it, thus highlighting it. This is followed by tapping the **ENTER** key once, which will immediately bring you to a menu where you are asked to enter the term that you wish to search. You then proceed by typing in the term or phrase.

Begin by selecting the first term/phrase from the three major concepts in your search request: foreign relations. You will find that this may be searched either as a phrase or a term. For this example, use the field **Descriptor-by keyword** and type in the phrase *foreign relations*.

Your search set will be given a number, one for the first set, two for the second and so on. When your first search is successful, you will need to begin your second search. You will be presented with the following screen when you have completed each of the three searches:

SET	#FOUND	(Page 1 of 1)
1	3738	Descriptors–keyword: FOREIGN RELATIONS
2	4112	Descriptors–keyword: UNITED STATES
3	29515	Descriptors–keyword: AUSTRALIA

The above search session retrieved a large number of records for each of the terms searched. The next step in the search process is to combine the above result sets using the **AND** operator.

First, you must select the Sets menu by tapping the **F5** key. This action presents you with a "pull down menu" from which you need to select the Combine Sets option. To select the option, use your down arrow key to highlight the option Combine sets and tap the **ENTER** key. You will now be presented with another pull down menu. The first option is Combine With AND and, as this option is already highlighted, you need only tap the **ENTER** key. You must now type in the set numbers that you want to combine with the **AND** operator. In this example you will combine sets 1 and 2 and 3, and after typing in **3** you must again tap the **ENTER** Key. You will now be presented with a menu that asks you to name the new set.

The new set will be the one that contains the three concepts that you begin with: foreign relations, United States, and Australia. It is important to give the set a *meaningful* name that reflects its contents, for example, FR,US&AUST. This will allow you to identify the set easily if further combinations are required. The above result set still contains a large number of records, 507 to be exact. This allows you to be even more precise and include your fourth option. Use the term 1990 to restrict your search to only those records containing 1990 in the source field.

To include 1990 you need to tap the **F3** key to use the Select menu. You will find that the highlighted option is the one you used last time, the **Descriptor-by keyword** option, so you will need to use the up arrow key to highlight the **Source** option and then tap the **ENTER** key. At this point you are presented with the Source menu that asks you to enter your term/phrase. Type in 1990 and tap the **ENTER** key.

This action will create a fifth set for the search on 1990 in the source field. To continue your search you now need to combine the set FR,US&AUST and set 5 (1990) using the **AND** operator. The procedure is the same as before: select the Sets menu by tapping the F5 key and select the Combine Sets option from the menu. This action brings you to the Combine Sets menu where you will select the Combine With AND option and combine the two sets (set 4 and set 5). You are again required to name the new set and you are advised to give it a meaningful name; for example, 90, FRUS&AUST. The result of this combination, 1990(source) AND Foreign Relations AND United States AND Australia is eight records in the result set. You will find that each record contains each of the *terms* you requested and in the fields you nominated.

The following three sample records are from the above search:[1]

RECORD #1 OF 8

TITLE	A review of key defence opinion polls in the 1980s
AUTHOR	MARSHALL, Alistair
SOURCE	Defence Force Journal, no.84, Sept/ Oct 1990 : (23)-28
INPUT DATE	9104
NOTES	bibl., tables
DESCRIPTORS	Surveys; Attitudes; United States: Foreign rela-

---

1. Reprinted with permission from AUSTROM.

	tions; International relation{; Australia: Defences; Armed forces
NUMBER	A91044084

RECORD #2 OF 8

TITLE	Australia and the Asian/Pacific region: recent developments
AUTHOR	DALTON, John
SOURCE	In: New Horizons in Politics: Essays with an Australian Focus (1990) : 132-149
INPUT DATE	9103
DESCRIPTORS	Defences; Commerce; United States: Defences; International aid; Australia: Foreign relations; Asia: Foreign relations; Pacific Ocean region: Foreign relations
NUMBER	A91032278

RECORD #6 OF 8

TITLE	Over-reach in Australia's regional military policy. [Version of paper presented at the Victorian Association for Peace Studies' conference 'The New Australian Militarism', Melbourne, Mar 1989]
AUTHOR	CHEESEMAN, Graeme
SOURCE	In: The New Australian Militarism: Undermining Our Future Security (1990): 73-92
INPUT DATE	9010
NOTES	illus., bibl
DESCRIPTORS	Pacific Ocean region; Southeast Asia; Armed forces; United States: Foreign relations; Australia: Foreign relations; Australia: Defences
IDENTIFIERS	Dibb, Paul. Review of Australia's Defence Capabilities (1986) (Dibb Report); Beazley, Kim; The Defence of Australia 198? (White Paper)
NUMBER	A901012719

To view the records, you will need to select the Display option from the Sets menu, Highlight the Display option and tap the **ENTER** key.

The next step is to indicate which set you wish to display. The set you need to select is the last set created which, in this case, is set 6. At this point you will be asked in what order you wish to display the records. The options that you are offered include:

> DISPLAY BY DEFAULT ORDER
> DISPLAY BY TITLE
> DISPLAY BY AUTHOR
> DISPLAY BY INPUT DATE
> DISPLAY BY INPUT DATE–REVERSE ORDER

The default order will suffice for this example. You are now able to view the first of the 8 records that your search retrieved. To view the remaining records you need to use the sideways arrow key by tapping it once. Tapping the sideways arrow key once again will allow you to view the third record and so on.

Boolean Searching on AUSTROM

The AND operator

To demonstrate the **AND** search the database LEISURE has been selected. The topic chosen for this search is fishing off Australia's Great Barrier Reef.

Begin by identifying the key concepts or terms in the research topic. The first term comes from the activity that you wish to undertake (i.e., fishing). The second term comes from the location or place that you wish to fish (i.e., Australia's Great Barrier Reef). So, to begin the search you will want to combine these two terms. To combine terms you must use the **AND** operator.

In AUSTROM there are two basic approaches that will allow you to combine two terms. The first is to search on each term separately and then combine the sets. The second method is to put both terms together in a single search statement (e.g., Fishing and Great Barrier Reef). There are, however, several advantages to searching each term separately and combining them later. The advantages include greater flexibility and control, especially if alternate terms are used in subsequent searches to gain greater precision. In an AUSTROM search, when a Boolean operator is used between two terms in a single search statement, the operator only acts on the first term following the operator. Furthermore, if you wish to choose to search on different fields with each of the terms, you will need to search the terms separately. Thus, unless you want an extremely simple search, *always* search on the terms separately with AUSTROM databases and do your combinations later.

Consider the following searches.

Fishing AND Great Barrier Reef

SET   #FOUND

1   11

The above search retrieves 11 records when searched on the Cross Search option. The Cross Search option is useful in that it searches every field of the record.

An examination of the records shows that one of the records does not contain any information about the Great Barrier Reef; only the terms *Fishing* and *Great* were searched for, so the program only acted on the first term following the search operator. While 10 out of 11 records may seem like a fairly precise recall, the results could have been much worse if a more common term had been selected.

If you again select the Cross Search option from the select menu, search first on the term *fishing*, and then separately for the term/phrase *Great Barrier Reef*, you will get the following results:

SET   #FOUND

1   288   Cross Search: Fishing
2   112   Cross Search: Great Barrier Reef

The above is only the first step. You will now need to combine the sets using the **AND** operator. To do this, you will need to tap the **F5** key to use the Set menu. Using the down arrow key, move the cursor to the option that allows you to combine sets and tap the

ENTER key. You are now given the choice of combining with **AND**, **OR**, or **NOT**. Select the **AND**. The program will now ask you to identify the set numbers that you wish to combine. To finish this operation tap the **ENTER** key. When the search is complete, you will be asked to "name" the search. (This is an important operation and one that needs a decision on your part.) The best approach is to select a meaningful name that will tell you something about the content of the set. For example *GBRfishing* is an appropriate name in this case. You will reach the following screen when you complete the search:

SET	#FOUND	
1	288	Cross Search: Fishing
2	112	Cross Search: Great Barrier Reef
3	10	COMBINE:GBR-FISHING

You will find that ten records are retrieved from the above search and that each record contains both the term *fishing* and the term/phrase *Great Barrier Reef*.

Examine the following three records:[2]

RECORD #1 OF 10

TITLE	Hey doc, let's go fishing
AUTHOR	Ellis G
PUB. TYPE	Book; Basic
NOTES	152 pages; ISBN 072701546X
DESCRIPTORS	Fishing; History; Anecdotes
IDENTIFIERS	Great Barrier Reef
NUMBER	2106

RECORD #2 OF 10

TITLE	Australia's Great Barrier Reef
AUTHOR	Endean R
DATE	1982
PUB. TYPE	Book; Intermediate

---

2. Reprinted with permission from AUSTROM.

ABSTRACT
A definitive book on the Great Barrier Reef covering the groups of animals and plants of the reef area, as well as many of the recent advances in understanding of major ecological problems relating to them. Includes topics such as the importance and the future of the reef, geography, topography, geology mode of formation, recent history, tourist resorts, fishing, reef walking, diving, strange and dangerous animals and the pressing need for conservation of fauna and flora.
NOTES 348 pages; ISBN 070221678X
DESCRIPTORS Ecology; Marine park; Biology; Natural resources; Flora; Conservation; Geography; Tourism; History
IDENTIFIERS Great Barrier Reef, Queensland
NUMBER 11799

RECORD #3 OF 10

TITLE The Great Barrier Reef: a regional case of tourism and natural resources
AUTHOR Tisdell C
SOURCE Australian Parks and Recreation, pages 37-42
DATE May 1983
PUB. TYPE Journal article; Intermediate
ABSTRACT
Important from an ecological standpoint, the Great Barrier Reef is also of economic significance. It supports substantial fishing and tourism industries. Partly in response to fears that oil mining might commence on the reef, the Great Barrier Reef Marine Park Act was passed in 1975. Whilst the Act has resolved a number of problems, conflict of interest still exists and there is scope for a greater input by economists into this area of natural resource management.
NOTES 10 references
DESCRIPTORS Environment; Natural resources; Tourism; Resort; National park; Economics; Zoning; Administration; Planning
IDENTIFIERS Great Barrier Reef, Queensland
NUMBER 11427

In these records both the terms/phrases that you searched on can be located in each record. In the records you can see that the phrase *Great Barrier Reef* is found in each case in the identifier field. You will remember that the identifier field is used for subject terms or place names that are not in the thesaurus or controlled vocabulary of the database but are "added" to the record to enhance subject access to the record. You are able to retrieve the above records because Cross Search was selected and Cross Search searches all of the record's fields.

Two other important fields to note are the field labelled **SOURCE** and the field labelled **PUB. TYPE**. It is the **SOURCE** field that is the key to locating the item. For example, in record 3 the field **PUB. TYPE** tells you that it is a journal article and the **SOURCE** field tells you that the article may be found in Australian Parks and Recreation, pages 37-42. You need to go one step further and take note of the information in the **DATE** field to establish the date of the journal issue that you seek; in this case it is May 1983.

In the other two records, the **PUB. TYPE** field shows that the publication is a book. To locate a book you will need to identify the book's author and title. If you examine the records you will see that each contains separate fields for the author and title.

The OR Operator

To demonstrate the **OR** operator the Australian Affairs Information Service database APAIS has been selected. This time the example will start with the **OR** search and then combine the **OR** search with the **AND** operator.

The search topic is concerned with Australia's military role in the Gulf conflict. You can begin your analysis of the question by identifying the key concepts or terms of the topic.

The first concept comes from the geographic region that you wish to identify. In this case at least two terms/phrases are appropriate:

1. MIDDLE EAST
2. GULF

The second concept comes from the group whose involvement you wish to identify. In this case several terms/phrases are appropriate:

1. Australian Troops
2. Australian Forces
3. Australian Navy
4. Australian Military

So, to begin the search you will want to combine the like or similar terms/phrases with the **OR** operator.

In AUSTROM the best approach is to conduct the searches separately and later combine the sets. When the terms/phrases are searched separately using the Cross Search option, the following result is achieved:

SET	#FOUND	
1	44	Cross Search: Gulf War
2	495	Cross Search: Middle East
3	15	Cross Search: Australian Troops
4	444	Cross Search: Australian Forces
5	389	Cross Search: Australian Navy
6	536	Cross Search: Australian Military

This is only the first step, as you will now need to combine the sets using the **OR** operator. To do this, tap the **F5** key to use the Set menu. Using the down arrow key, move the cursor to the option that allows you to combine sets and tap the **ENTER** key. You are now given the choice of combining with **AND**, **OR**, or **NOT**: select **OR**. The program will now ask you to identify the set numbers that you wish to combine. Type in each of the set numbers that you wish to associate with the **OR** operator, sets 1 and 2. You need to repeat the procedure with the sets 3, 4, 5, and 6. To finish this procedure, tap the **ENTER** key.

When the search is complete, you will be asked to "name" the search. This is an important operation and one that needs a decision on your part. The best approach is to select a meaningful name that will tell you something about the content of the set.

To review the procedure follow the steps below:

1. Tap **F5** and select **COMBINE SETS**.
2. Select the **OR** operator.

3. Identify the sets that you wish to combine (**1 OR 2**).
4. Name the new set (**mideast**).

Now repeat the above operation with sets 3, 4, 5, and 6 and name your new set (**AUST TROOPS**).

You should now have two new sets that you created which are, in fact, combinations of the above list of sets.

SET	#FOUND	
1	44	Cross Search: Gulf War
2	495	Cross Search: Middle East
3	15	Cross Search: Australian Troops
4	444	Cross Search: Australian Forces
5	389	Cross Search: Australian Navy
6	536	Cross Search: Australian Military
7	**515**	**COMBINE: MIDEAST**
8	**1080**	**COMBINE: AUST-TROOPS**

To finish off your query, you should now combine the two new sets with the **AND** operator. This combination will bring the two concepts of your search together and greatly reduce the number of documents retrieved. Combining set 7 and set 8 from the above screen will give you the following result set:

SET	#FOUND	
9	7	COMBINE: AUST-GULF

Examine the following three records for occurrences of the terms that you searched on.[3]

RECORD #1 OF 7

TITLE	PM's 'bon voyage' to sailors for the Gulf. [Address by the Prime Minister at the departure of the Royal Australian Navy contribution to the Gulf multinational force, Sydney, 13 Aug 1990]
AUTHOR	HAWKE, Bob
SOURCE	Australian Foreign Affairs and Trade, v.61, no.8, Aug 1990 : 482-483

---

3. Reprinted with permission from AUSTROM.

INPUT DATE	9105
NOTES	ports
DESCRIPTORS	Navies; War
IDENTIFIERS	HMAS Darwin; Gulf War 1991
NUMBER	A91054758

RECORD #2 OF 7

TITLE	Fears of a fifth column. [Threat of terrorism in Australia because of it{' military participation in the Gulf]
AUTHOR	LIPSON, Norm
SOURCE	Bulletin (Sydney), 22 Jan 1991 : 24-25
INPUT DATE	9104
NOTES	col. illus
DESCRIPTORS	Islam; Middle East: Politics and government; Risk; Jews; Terrorism; Security; Intelligence services
IDENTIFIERS	Surveillance; Hussein, Saddam; Iraq; Australian Security Intelligence Organization
NUMBER	A91043683

RECORD #3 OF 7

TITLE	The peacekeepers: experiences of Australian personnel
AUTHOR	WEBSTER, Anthony; MEEKIN, Steve and WARREN, Richard
SOURCE	In: Australia and Peacekeeping (1990) : (61)-75
INPUT DATE	9104
DESCRIPTORS	Armed forces; Middle East: Defences; Africa: Defences
IDENTIFIERS	Australia. Australian Defence Force; United Nations Truce Supervision Organization (UNSTO); United Nations Iran/Iraq Military Observer Group (UNIIMOG); United Nations Transition Assistance Group (UNTAG); Namibia
NUMBER	A91043773

The *NOT* Operator

The **NOT** operator is used to exclude terms/phrases from your search. It is called a limiting or restricting operator. The **NOT** operator is probably the least commonly used of the Boolean operators, but it is still an effective tool.

The simplest use of a **NOT** operator would be by itself in a search statement, for example:

females NOT males

A more common use would be in conjunction with the other Boolean operators, particularly the **AND** operator. Consider the following question. In this example, you are interested in violence in men's prisons in Australia, but not in women's prisons.

To begin, you will need to identify the concepts that exist in this search topic. For example:

Concept 1   prison

Concept 2   men

Concept 3   violence

Concept 4   Australia

Concept 5   women

You also need to identify equivalent terms for each of the concepts. Prison could be combined with Jail using the **OR** operator. Men could be combined with Male using the **OR** operator. Finally, the term Women could be combined with the term Female using the **OR** operator. Each of the concept groups will need to be linked by the **AND** operator. When this is complete, you may now effectively use the **NOT** operator to exclude terms that you wish to exclude from your result, for this example, **Women OR Female**.

The next step before starting your search is to select a suitable database on which to conduct your search. The database selected in this instance is the Australian Criminology Database (CINCH). As the search will be conducted on an Australian database, it is not necessary to search on the term Australia.

The following searches will be conducted using Cross Search so that each of the record's fields will be searched. As this search will only involve two terms in the initial part of the search, the **OR** combinations will be entered into the search statement.

To begin, tap the **F3** function key, and use the down arrow key to select the Cross Search option, and tap the **ENTER** key. This will immediately bring you to the menu that asks you to type in your search request **PRISON OR JAIL**. Tapping the **ENTER** key will signal the program to search on your request. Repeat the procedure for the remaining two searches. Your screen should give you the following results:

SET	#FOUND	
1	1046	Cross Search: PRISON OR JAIL
2	209	Cross Search: MEN OR MALE
3	803	Cross Search: VIOLENCE
4	635	Cross Search: WOMEN OR FEMALE

You will now need to link the first three sets with the **AND** operator. To link the sets, tap the **F5** key to reveal the Sets menu. Then use your down arrow key to highlight the Combine Sets option and tap the **ENTER** key. Select the Combine With AND option and combine the sets 1, 2, and 3. You will now be requested to name the new set; again, a meaningful choice is advised. For example, PRIS.VIOL will be given in this case.

To finish, you will now need to exclude the concept Female by linking set 5 (PRIS.VIOL) and set 4 using the **NOT** operator. To link the sets, tap the **F5** key and select the Combine Sets option. Select the Combine With NOT option and enter set 5 followed by set 4. Note the order is important because you want to include set 5 (PRIS.VIOL) and exclude set 4 (Women or Female). The result set obtained by excluding set 4 resulted in a set with fewer records than the set PRIS.VIOL, as the terms *Women* and *Female* will have been excluded. The result set in this case contained 32 records. The following record is a sample from this search.[4]

---

4. Reprinted with permission from AUSTROM.

RECORD #1 OF 32

TITLE	Classification 'G', Intractable: the prison perspective on violence
AUTHOR	Matthews, Bernie
SOURCE	Criminology Australia, 1(4) Apr/May 1990; 12
PUBLICATION TYPE	Article
ABSTRACT	Brief extract from paper delivered at the National Conference on Violence, 10-13 October 1989
DESCRIPTORS	Effects of imprisonment; Prison management; Corrections policies
MINOR DESCRIPTORS	Correctional planning; Rehabilitation; Effects of imprisonment; Violent inmates; Inmate attitudes
GEOG. IDENTIFIERS	Grafton; New South Wales
NAMES	Grafton Gaol; Royal Commission into New South Wales Prisons; Nagle, John Flood, Royal Commissioner
NUMBER	02274590041990

DOWNLOADING RECORDS

The procedure for downloading records in AUSTROM is fairly straightforward. You need to start by tapping **F5** to present the sets menu. Then use your down arrow key to highlight the *Export a Set* command and tap the **ENTER** key. At this point the program will request that you type in the set number that you wish to download. In this example use the last one that you created on violence in prisons. You will be given the choice between the following 3 options:

>Comma Delimited
>Fixed Field
>Print to Disc

The third option, *Print to Disc*, is the most suitable format for use with word processing software. The first option, *Comma Delimited*, is suitable for retrieval by database programs such as ProCite. After deciding the format, you will be given the option of downloading the records in one of the three following orders:

>Save by Default Order
>Save by Author
>Save by Title

After deciding on the order in which you wish to download the records, you must decide if you wish to download the entire record, a short record, or a user-selected output. In most cases you should download the entire record. The last step is the most important since you must now choose the path and the name of the file that you will create. The path is the place or disc and directory that you wish to send the file to; for example, **A:\datafile\prison.doc**, where **A** is the drive, **\datafile** is the subdirectory, and **prison.doc** is the file name. You must take care in this operation or you will lose your information.

PRINTING RECORDS

The procedure for printing records in AUSTROM is similar to that for downloading records. The first step is to tap the **F5** key to present the Sets menu. Then use your down arrow key to highlight the Print a Set command and tap the **ENTER** key. At this point the program will request that you type in the set number that you wish to print. After entering in the set number you will be given the option of printing out the set in one of the three following orders:

>Print by Default Order
>Print by Author
>Print by Title

After deciding the order in which you wish to print, you are able to print out either the entire record, a short record, or a user-defined record. In most cases, it is wise to print out the entire record.

Chapter 11

Grolier Encyclopedia

THE NEW GROLIER ELECTRONIC ENCYCLOPEDIA

The New Grolier Electronic Encyclopedia is a full-text database containing the complete 21 volumes of the Academic American Encyclopedia on a single CD ROM. In addition to giving you a vast amount of information in a compact form, you are also given all the retrieval power of Boolean logic. The combination of Boolean searching and full-text retrieval gives you ready access to over 9 million words and 30,000 articles in electronic form. The material contained in the dictionary includes images as well as text, and you can search a picture index for specific images.

FULL-TEXT SEARCHING

The advantage of full-text searching is that it enables you to retrieve the actual information you request. Unlike bibliographic databases that only provide references to material on your subject, full-text databases are at once a retrieval tool and a supplier of information. For example, a search on **trout** retrieves over 50 articles about that fish. In fact, a look at the first article reveals that pictures of the fish are available. With the touch of two keys you can retrieve a color picture of two rainbow trout.

A number of menus are provided to allow easy access to information contained odisc. From the first menu (shown below), you are able to select from three options.

ALT\ File Edit Tools Windows Options   Help

SEARCH CHOICE

You can either begin a search or get HELP on how to use the encyclopedia.
Highlight your choice and press ENTER

New Search:
Word Search
Browse Titles
Browse Word Index

The Word Index is actually an alphabetical listing of every word in the database. To use the Browse Word Index option, you need to highlight your selection and tap the **ENTER** key once. The next step is to type in the term that you wish to search for at the Browse Word Index screen. For example, if you choose to use the Browse Word Index to search for information on the inventor Thomas Edison, you need to type in the term Edison at the Browse Word Index screen. This will bring you to the point in the Word Index where **Edison** is found. If you tap the **ENTER** key again (to select the highlighted term Edison) you will be brought to the next list, which will present **Edison, Thomas Alva**, the inventor. If you tap the **ENTER** key while his name is highlighted, you will retrieve the first article about him.

The Browse Titles index allows you to search for keywords found in article titles. Searching in the article titles is a very restricted form of searching. The reason for searching within a title may be to recall an article that you previously used or one that you have a reference to. Titles should not be searched as a subject entry in a full-text database unless you are finding huge amounts of information in the Word Index and need to restrict your search. Even then, you are better advised to use the Word Search option and to control your search with the use of Boolean operators rather than just searching the title field.

The Word Search option is the most powerful and flexible form of searching offered by the New Grolier Electronic Encyclopedia. The details of Word Search will be covered later under Advanced Searching Techniques. It is important that you master the Word Search to take full advantage of the material available in this product.

PICTURE RETRIEVAL

The New Grolier Electronic Encyclopedia allows searching for images via a picture index. To use the picture index, you need to tap the **ALT** key and the **I** key simultaneously. This will bring you to a list of topics arranged in alphabetical order of the pictures held. To obtain a picture, you need to highlight your selection and tap the **ENTER** key. For example, if you do a search on the term *ship*, you will be presented with a list of terms with the term *ship* highlighted. To continue, you need to tap the **ENTER** key and you will be shown a selection of ships ranging from a birch bark canoe to a Viking longship. To retrieve the actual ship image of your choice, you need only to highlight your selection and tap the **ENTER** key. This action will retrieve a picture of the ship that you selected.

The picture index is quite extensive and very interesting. In addition to objects there are pictures of animals, plants, and people. If, for example, you are doing research on a particular variety of flower, you will be able to retrieve both information about the flower and a picture of the flower. The pictures are frequently associated with a particular article.

As the article on Edison has a picture associated with it, you are able to retrieve his picture as well. To retrieve the picture, you need to tap the **ALT** key and the **3** key simultaneously.

ADVANCED SEARCHING TECHNIQUES

The first menu that you are presented with gives you three search options: Word Search, Browse Titles and Browse Word Index. The Word Search option is the most advanced of the three search options. It allows you to search on either single terms/phrases or a combination of terms/phrases. Your initial search screen is shown below:

[WORD SEARCH]

Type search word or words then select BEGIN SEARCH and press ENTER.

```
Word(s)  [                                              >
with     [                                              >
with     [                                              >
with     [                                              >
```

BEGIN SEARCH

To search you need only type your term/phrase in the first line and tap the **ENTER** key twice. You will be presented with an option to View Titles. To select the option View Titles, again tap the **ENTER** key once. This brings you to a list of titles from which you can select a title by highlighting it and tapping the **ENTER** key. You will find that you are now presented with the full-text of the article. To move within the article you need to use the arrow keys. Alternatively, you are able to move from each occurrence of your search term/phrase by tapping the **TAB** key. To return to your title list, you need to tap the **ESCAPE** key. Tapping the Escape key will always take you back one step. Thus, tapping the **ESCAPE** key once from the title list returns you to the Search menu.

Searching the New Grolier Electronic Encyclopedia is accomplished via a number of menus. These menus need to be examined before effective searching can take place. The menu option **O** for Options allows you to use the menus to gain control over your search. To access the menu, you need to tap the **ALT** key and the **O** key simultaneously. This will cause the Option menu to be displayed. The Option menu works with the initial Search menu shown above. That is, the changes or selections that you make with the Options menu interact with specific terms or phrases that have been typed in the initial menu.

Below is an illustration of the Search Options menu:

Search Options–
Search In:
- Article Titles
- Article Text
- Picture Captions
- Bibliographies
- Factboxes

Word Relationship:
    In Same Article
- In Same Paragraph
    Words Apart [#]
    Exact Order

    Negate Search Line

Consider how the menu is used in the following exercise. In this exercise you are searching for information about the natural flooding of the two major rivers that run from Tibet through China: the Yangtze and the Yellow Rivers. The Yellow River is also known by the name *Hwang Ho* and you will need to include references to the Hwang Ho. You may also choose to restrict the search by eliminating the term *farming* to exclude man-made flooding from your search, and you will need to use the equivalent of the **NOT** operator to exclude those references that relate to farming.

You will need to start by breaking down the question into its component concepts, for example:

Concept 1 (China, Tibet)

Concept 2 (Yellow River, Hwang Ho, Yangtze)

Concept 3 (Flooding)

Concept 4 (Farming)

Concept 1 (China and Tibet) contains two terms and a comma, the equivalent of the **OR** operator. The comma must be used so that either term will be retrieved. Concept 2 also contains two terms (Yellow River and Yangtze), and Yellow River has an alternative name, Hwang Ho. Concept 3 (Flooding) is complete in itself and does not need any alternative terms. Concept 4 (Farming) can be expanded by adding the term Agriculture and linking it to the term *farming* using the equivalent of the **OR** operator.

Now that the concepts have been examined, you will need to consider how you will link the concepts to achieve your answer. Basically you will want to link concepts 1 and 2 and 3 with the **AND** operator, and exclude concept 3 by using the **NOT** operator.

To carry out this search strategy, you will need to make use of the menu searching techniques that are used by the New Grolier Electronic Encyclopedia. Refer to the Search Option menu above for reference.

Consider the following steps:

Step 1   Type **China,Tibet** in the first line of the Word Search screen.

Step 2   Type **Yangtze, Yellow River, Hwang Ho** in the second line of the Word Search screen.

Step 3   Type **Flooding** in the third line of the Word Search screen.

Step 4   Tap the **ALT** key and the **O** key simultaneously to access the Search Option menu. Confirm that the search settings (indicated by the • (dot) preceding the option) are correct before continuing.

Step 5   Highlight the last option in the Search Option menu, Negate Search Line, and tap the **ENTER** key once. The fourth line of the Word Search menu should now say **NOT with.**

Step 6   To leave the Option menu, tap the **ESCAPE** key once. Type in the terms **Farming, Agriculture** in the third line of the Word Search menu.

Note that in the above search screen the **AND** operator is assumed between the first and second and third lines. Thus, concept 1

(China and Tibet) is linked with the terms on the second line, concept 2 (Yellow River and Hwang Ho and Yangtze), and to the term on the third line, concept 3, (Flooding), by the Boolean operator **AND**. The terms located within the first, second, and fourth lines are linked by the equivalent **OR** operator, comma. The comma placed between the two terms functions as an **OR** operator so that either of the terms is retrieved. The terms/phrases on the fourth line (Farming and Agriculture) will be excluded from the search by the **NOT** operator.

There are two final checks to make before proceeding with the search. The first is to examine what fields you wish to search in. You need to tap the **ALT** key and **O** key simultaneously to retrieve the Search Options menu.

Now you are given the choice of searching in one, all, or a combination of the fields listed in the Search Options menu. Therefore you may choose from any combination of the following fields:

- Article Titles
- Article Text
- Picture Captions
- Bibliographies
- Factboxes

The dot to the left of the field indicates that the field will be searched. To exclude a field from the search, you need to highlight the field and tap the **ENTER** key once. Similarly, to include a field, you need to highlight the field and tap the **ENTER** key once.

The second check is also made from the Options menu. You need to indicate the sections of the records that you wish to search. You are able to choose among the following record segments:

- In Same Article
  In Same Paragraph
  Words Apart [ ]
  Exact Order

In the first instance, selecting **In the Same Article** will search the entire article for the terms you requested and check that each of the terms reside in the same article. The second search option, **In**

the Same Paragraph, requires that each of the terms that you requested reside in the same paragraph. The third search option allows you to assign any number of words within which your search terms must reside. The final option, **Exact Order**, allows you to have the terms you enter searched in the exact order that you have typed them in.

To continue your search and leave the Search Options menu tap the **ESCAPE** key once and tap the **ENTER** key once to proceed with the search. After the search is complete you are requested to View Titles and you must tap the **ENTER** key again. This search retrieved 4 titles/articles on the topic. To view the title list you may use either the down arrow key or the **PgDn** key to travel down the list of titles. To view an article you must highlight your selection and tap the **ENTER** key once.

The example given below is located under the title "Hwang Ho":[1]

The Hwang Ho, or Yellow River, is the second longest river (after the Yangtze) in China. Flowing generally east from the Tibetan Highlands to the Yellow Sea in north China, it has a length of 4,830 km (3,000 mi). Its drainage area is more than 750,800 sq km (290,000 sq mi), encompassing 20 million ha (49.5 million acres) farmland and a population of more than 100 million. The river received its name because its unusually high silt content (mainly loess soil) gives it a yellowish appearance. The river is known as the "sorrow of China" because of its frequent, and often catastrophic, flooding.

The volume of traffic is very small because the river is shallow and parts of its lower course are choked with ice during December and January. Principal cities on the Hwang Ho include Tsinan (Chinan), K'AI-FENG, CHENG-CHOU, Lo-yang, SIAN, Pao-t'ou, and LAN-CHOU. Since 1955 the government has undertaken a comprehensive multipurpose water-conservation project to harness this historically flood-prone river. Two of the largest multipurpose dams constructed along its course are the Liu-chia Station, near Lan-

---

1. Reprinted with permission from The Electronic Encyclopedia (TM) (c) 1990 Grolier Electronic Publishing, Inc.

chou, and the San-men Station, west of Lo-yang. Each produces more than 1 million kw of electricity.

Environment

The average annual precipitation in the Hwang Ho basin is only about 400 mm (16 in). However, both the seasonal occurrence and the annual amount of rainfall in northern China vary greatly, creating a wide disparity in river flow. The average annual discharge of 48 km(3) (11 mi(3)) is only about one-twentieth that of the Yangtze River. There are two major high-water periods (spring and late summer) and two low-water seasons (early summer and winter).

In its upper course the Hwang Ho flows generally northeast. Its middle course describes an enormous rectangular incursion into Inner Mongolia, then flows south, where it cuts through the Loess Plateau. The river's water is clean in the upper and upper-middle course, but when it passes through the easily erodable loess of Shansi and Shensi provinces, it picks up the bulk of the 1,440,000 metric tons (1,600 million U.S. tons) of sediments it carries in one year.

The lower course begins at Tun-kuan, where the river turns east and flows across the North China Plain to the Yellow Sea. Here the river is elevated 3 to 10 m (10 to 33 ft) above the surrounding lowland. For a distance of 1,800 km (1,120 mi) the river is encased by artificial embankments to prevent disastrous flooding.

The gradient of the river in the upper and middle courses is steep–about 2 m per km (10 ft per mi). The lower course has a much less steep gradient of 4 cm per km (2.5 in per mi), and the slower-flowing river tends to deposit much of its sediments–thus creating the elevated riverbed. The high silt content makes the Hwang Ho delta the fastest growing delta in the world. Each year it extends 2 km (1.2 mi) farther into the sea.

History

The middle course of the Hwang Ho, particularly Honan province, with its fertile river-deposited soils, was the homeland of China's ancient civilization. Since the 3d millennium BC, there have been 26 course changes (9 of them major ones) recorded for the Hwang Ho. In the same period it breached its dikes more than 1,500 times. The last major change in course occurred in 1947, when the river, which had been flowing south to the Yellow Sea through Kansu since 1938, retook its northern route to the Gulf of Chihli. As a result of numerous waterworks on the Hwang Ho built since the 1950s, no major floods have occurred along the river in the last two decades.

James Chan

Bibliography:

Sinclair, Kevin, The Yellow River (1987).

SPECIAL FEATURES

The New Grolier Electronic Encyclopedia has a number of features that are unique to ondisc retrieval systems.

Pull-Down Menus

The first is the arrangement of "Pull-down menus." This feature will be familiar to you if you are accustomed to word processor or spreadsheet software that uses a similar approach. The key to using the pull-down menus is to press the highlighted letter and the **ALT** key simultaneously. The pull-down menu is the means through which all the other special features are accessed. The following are some examples of these features.

NotePad (Downloading/Printing)

NotePad is a feature that allows you to organize your research for later reference or printing. To use the NotePad feature you must do the following.

First mark the text that you wish to save by tapping the **ALT** and

M keys simultaneously and by using your down arrow key to actually mark the actual text.

Second, when you have finished marking the text that you wish to save, you must tap the **ALT** and the **C** key simultaneously to move the text to the NotePad. A message will confirm that the text has in fact been saved to the NotePad.

You are now able to either continue your search or exit and work with the text you have saved to the NotePad. You must remember to save the NotePad prior to exiting by tapping the **ALT** and **F** key simultaneously. At this point you will need to highlight the Save NotePad Option and tap the **ENTER** key.

The final step is to give the file a name and, again, a meaningful name will assist you in recalling the document later. This approach is useful in that you are able to upload the document into a word processor if you wish.

An alternative method of using the information that you have retrieved is to print it directly from the NotePad. The procedure is similar to the above in that you must: (1) Mark the text, (2) Copy the text to the NotePad.

The next step is to access the Print Menu, by tapping the **ALT** and **P** keys simultaneously. You will need to highlight the options that you select before highlighting the Begin Printing option. The text that you have selected will be printed immediately.

It is always to your advantage to save the text to a file and do the printing later via a word processor. This will allow you to edit the material and to include other material with it.

BookMarks

The BookMarks feature is extremely easy to use and, if used properly, will save you a considerable amount of time. This feature is used from within an article; that is, when you are viewing a text. It works in conjunction with the NotePad feature in that the references that the BookMarks feature creates are saved to the NotePad. To create a reference using this feature you need only tap the **ALT** and **B** keys simultaneously. After the creation of each BookMark, the saving of the BookMarks will be confirmed. You are now able to use the saved BookMarks in any of the ways that you would use other NotePad material.

The BookMarks feature is extremely useful since it allows you to save references to articles without interrupting your search. Thus you can record references, carry on with your search, and leave your review to the last.

Link

Link is a feature that allows you to move from See Also References that exist in an article. To use Link you must tap the **ALT** and **L** keys simultaneously. This results in your cursor being moved to the next occurrence of a See Also Reference.

Chapter 12

ISI® Citation Indexes– Social Sciences Citation Index® and Science Citation Index®

SOURCES OF INFORMATION

The two citation indexes, Science Citation Index® (SCI®) Compact Disc Edition and Social Sciences Citation Index® (SSCI®) Compact Disc Edition, form a multidisciplinary index to journal literature in science and social science respectively. SCI® indexes over 3,300 journals in over 100 scientific disciplines. The SSCI® indexes over 1,400 journals in the social sciences in over 50 disciplines.

The ISI® Citation Indexes can be used simply as conventional author and subject indexes or in a manner that makes them unique as citation indexes. That is, you can use the ISI® indexes to retrieve documents that *cite* a particular author's work.

The principle underlying citation indexing is the association or relationship between a document and the items that the document cites. This principle is taken a step further to include the association between two or more papers that cite the same document. This may seem complex, but after a few trial searches the relationship between documents and the documents cited by them and between documents that share common citations, will become clear.

The advantages of citation indexes come from their flexibility and power in searching. With citation indexes you can expect to find:

- locations of works that share common citations
- citations of a work
- reviews of a work
- documents searched by author, title, or journal.

If you know a specific author whose work is relevant to your research, you are able to retrieve recent documents that cite the known author's work. Thus you can readily locate recent material in your area of interest.

SEARCHING THE SOCIAL SCIENCES CITATION INDEX®

Note: The searches are only examples of searching strategies and not comprehensive searches.

The ISI® citation indexes are among the most useful and flexible of the ondisc products that you will encounter. ISI® indexes allow for precise use of Boolean logic and field qualifications. With ISI® citation indexes you are able to combine Boolean logic and field-specific searching to control your searches. Searching via citation indexes is more flexible than the other databases you have examined. With the ISI® Compact Disc Editions you are able to search a database by title, author, journal, address, and citation.

It may take slightly longer to be proficient in searching with ISI®, but as you become more familiar with the searching protocol, you will appreciate the precision and flexibility of this remarkable product.

Main Menu

Below is the first menu ISI® presents to you.

V3.04 Social Sciences Citation Index (Jan 92 - Mar 92) D3.0

F1-Help   F2-Database   F3-Search   F4-Results   F5-Quit

———————————Search Session———————————
Set Records Field

---

1   Title
         **Enter as single words or phrases: ENVIRONMEN-
         TAL or ENVIRONMENTAL IMPACT
         Press ENTER to execute search.**

Alt–Fields **ALT–D**ictionary **ALT–L**imit ALT–Undo ALT–Copy-Query
Alt–ClearSession ALT–PrintSession ALT–SaveStrategy **ALT–R**un-Strategy

Once you have selected the database that you will search, you need to tap the **F3** key to begin your search. To proceed you will need to select the field that you wish to search. The first, or default, option is the title field that allows you to search for terms found in the titles of all documents in the database. To select a field of your choice, tap the **ALT** key and the **F** key simultaneously. This action will retrieve the field selection menu. SSCI® gives you the choice of the following fields:

> **Title**
> **Author**
> **Citation**
> **Address**
> **Abbr Journal**
> **Full Journal**
> **Set**

To select the field that you wish to search on, for example the citation field, use the up and down arrow keys to highlight your choice (citation) and then tap the **ENTER** key.

The following search question will involve looking for work on technological diffusion theory. One of the major writers in diffusion theory is E. M. Rogers. He was one of the first writers in the area of diffusion of technology. By searching for authors who have cited his work you may be able to find more recent works on the same subject.

To begin your search, select the citation option from the list of fields. You will need to tap the **F** key and the **ALT** key simultaneously to retrieve the Field menu. Use the arrow key to highlight the Citation option and tap the **ENTER** key. You will be presented with a screen that asks you to type in the citation (cited author) that you intend to search on. You can now type in the surname of the cited author followed by a dash and then the author's initials:

Rogers-EM

This request for Rogers-EM as a cited author retrieves 64 records where Rogers is the first named author. To examine the records you need to tap the **F4** key and select one of the Show Results options. You are given the choice between showing the full record or just the record title.

The record below is a sample of a full record from the above request:[1]

Onkvisit-S Shaw-JJ

The Diffusion of Innovations Theory-Some Research Questions and Ideas
(English) => Article

AKRON BUSINESS AND ECONOMIC REVIEW
Vol 20 Iss 1 pp 46-55 1989 (T8058)

Related Records:18 References:30

RECORD STRUCTURE

As you can see, a cited reference search on Rogers-EM retrieved a paper on diffusion theory. Cited reference searching enables you to locate relevant papers without developing synonyms or title words. In this record, the full bibliographic details are shown. The first field of the record contains the authors' names. The first author is the principle author. Following the authors is the title, the language and document type, the source, and finally the number of Related Records™, and the number of references.

Tap **F** (references) to display the 30 references listed by Onkvi-

---

1. Reprinted with permission from ISI®.

sit and Shaw. The cited papers will display, with Rogers-EM as one of the cited papers. For example, the author's name may be searched to determine either what he/she has written (an author search) or as a citation to determine who has cited that author (a citation search). You may also search for a specific work by its title (a title search).

An effective approach to searching is to use one of the SSCI® dictionaries to identify your search terms, whether they are title words, cited authors, author addresses, cited works, author names, or journal titles. In the next section the Citation Dictionary and the title word search will be examined in-depth.

USING THE CITATION DICTIONARIES

The Dictionary option (**ALT-D**) will allow you to quickly view terms. This is perhaps the most user friendly option of the ISI® Compact Disc Editions in that it allows you to select your expression from a list after typing in the term or phrase that you intend to initially search on. The value of using the dictionary is that it enables you to see variant word endings or phrase-bound (hyphenated) items as in a cited reference search.

The dictionary is context-sensitive in that it will correspond to the type of search that you intend to make (i.e., if you are searching by title, the dictionary will default to a list of title words). The title dictionary lists alphabetically all the words in the title of each article, editorial, book review, or other document that the database indexes. Each field listed below has a dictionary option:

> **Title**
> **Author**
> **Citation**
> **Address**
> **Abbr Journal**
> **Full Journal**

The following example will use the title field and will access title dictionary terms. To begin, select the dictionary option by tapping the **D** key and the **ALT** keys at the same time. This will bring you into the list of title words. As you are at the beginning of the list you will need to type in the title or title words that you wish to retrieve.

For this example the term *diffusion* is typed in while the title list is present. The term is now highlighted in the title list. The title list will also show you the number of records that contain the term that you searched. In this case 25 records contain the term. You will also see any variant word endings above or below the term *diffusion*. You may want to add those terms to your search. Tap the **SPACE BAR** to select each variant term, then tap the **ENTER** key to transfer all these terms to the search query box. To proceed with the search tap the **ENTER** key twice. The search is complete when a set number has been given to the term and you are presented with a blank search screen.

To retrieve the records you need to tap the **F4** (results) key and choose to view either the record's title or the full record. The record below was retrieved from this title search:[2]

Ray-GF
Full Circle–The **Diffusion** of Technology (English) =>Article
RESEARCH POLICY
Vol 18 Iss 1 pp 1-18 1989 (U6705)
Related Records:4 REFERENCES:11

The retrieval of the first record or set of records may be only the beginning since the ISI® Citation Indexes allow a searcher to retrieve records *related* to the initial retrieval. For example, in the record below you will find that it has 20 Related Records™ and 29 references. Records are "related" if they have one or more bibliographic references in common. The more references in common, the higher the subject relationship between the two papers. **The Related Records™** feature enables you to "browse" literature and locate items that you did not initially search for.

---

2. Reprinted with permission from ISI®.

Parent

Trajtenberg-M Yitzhaki-S

The Diffusion of Innovations–A Methodological Reappraisal
(English) => Article

JOURNAL OF BUSINESS & ECONOMIC STATISTICS
Vol 7 Iss 1 pp 35-47 1989 (T3224)

Related Records:20 References:29

The above record is said to be the "Parent" record to the twenty records that it lists as Related Records™. The term "parent" does not imply a hierarchical relationship. It only indicates that in this instance it is the source of the Related Records™.

To view a Related Record™ you will need to tap the highlighted **R** key. In this case, you will retrieve 20 records. If you examine this record, you will note that it has Related Records™ and references as well. The record below is the first of the twenty Related Records™ retrieved.[3]

Related Record™ (level 1)

Mansfield-E

Technological-Change in Robotics–Japan and the United-States
(English) => Article

MANAGERIAL AND DECISION ECONOMICS
Iss NSI pp 19-25 1989 (U1093)

Related Records:12 References:21 Shared References:2

---

3. Reprinted with permission from ISI®.

One observable difference between a parent record and a Related Record™ is that the related record shows the number of references that it shares with its parent record. As you will notice, this paper by Mansfield-E also has Related Records™, 12 of them. To examine those records tap the **R** key. There are a maximum of five levels of Related Records™ available from the initial parent record. In this case the parent record is the paper by Trajtenberg-M and Yitzhaki-S. In order to see exactly which cited references Trajtenberg and Yitzhaki used in their paper and which cited references were used in Mansfield's paper, tap the **H** key (shared references). You will find that there are 2 cited references that *both* papers used in their bibliographies. To return to the original list of the records, you need to tap the **ESCAPE** key until you return to that screen.

The Related Records™ feature will allow you to continue retrieving Related Records™ of a parent record up to 5 times. That is, you can retrieve the Related Record™ of a Related Record™, and continue until the fifth occasion. The direct relevancy of the retrieved records will decrease in accordance with the level of the record.

This feature is useful if you are interested in tracking down everyone who is writing in a particular field. It can, however, retrieve a number of records with questionable relevancy if more than two levels of Related Records™ are searched.

To view a record's cited reference you need to tap the **F** key. This action will retrieve an alphabetical list of the document's 21 cited references.

Sample Reference

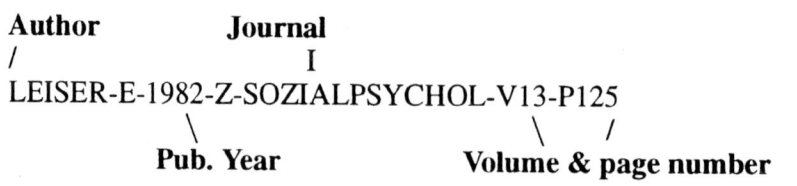

While looking at the cited references you may wish to see if anyone else has cited that document. To view how many times a particular reference was cited, you need to highlight that reference and tap the **ENTER** key. This action will also create a set from the reference that you highlighted. The reference itself, as a citation search, will become a set. To use the newly created set you must leave the reference display by tapping the **ESC** key and tap the **F3** key and then the **ENTER** key. You will be back at the Search Session box and your query will appear there as a numbered set. Move your highlight bar so that it is over this item and then tap the **F4** key (results) to see who else has cited Leiser-E's 1982 paper.

BOOLEAN SEARCHING

ISI® Citation Indexes can also support searching using Boolean logic, that is, searching using **AND, OR,** and **NOT** operators.

Consider the following example:

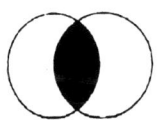

THE "AND" SEARCH

In this instance, you are looking for an article written on an aspect of technology by an author who you only know by his surname, Smith. As both the surname *Smith* and the term *technology* are extremely common, neither would be suitable for a search on its own. However, when you break the search query into its separate components, the creator or author of the document, Smith (concept 1), and the subject/title term, technology (concept 2), the search is workable. Combine the two concepts by selecting the terms *Smith* and *technology* and establish the relationship between them by using the **AND** operator.

To begin, tap the **F3** key and tap the **ENTER** key. You will then need to select your field by pressing the **ALT** and **F** keys simultaneously. This action will result in a list of searchable fields. Then use the arrow key to highlight the field you wish to select, the Author field, and tap the **ENTER** key. You are now presented with the menu that allows you to enter the author's surname, Smith. The authors named are automatically truncated. The result is the same as the application of a truncation symbol in that every occurrence of Smith is retrieved (484 records).

For the second half of your search you will need to select the Title field and search on the term *technology*. Searching on a term as common as technology retrieves a large number of records as well (496). You now have created two sets, one for the author, Smith, and one for the title, Technology. To combine the two sets you need to press the **ALT** key and the **F** key simultaneously and obtain the field list. Use the arrow key to highlight the field you wish to select (set) and tap the **ENTER** key. You are now presented with a menu that allows you to enter the sets that you wish to combine, that is, set 1 and set 2. You will need to type in numbers 1 and 2 with the **AND** operator between them (i.e., 1 AND 2), to obtain a set of records that will have an occurrence of the term *technology* in the title field and *Smith* in the author field. The combination of the two sets with the **AND** operator will create the new set, which contains only 3 records.

You will find that use of the **AND** operator between two terms always has the effect of narrowing the search and giving you a precise result.

The OR and NOT Operators

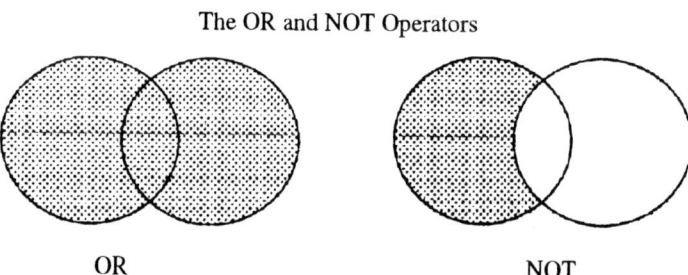

OR　　　　　　　　　　　　　NOT

In this instance, you are looking for a document(s) with either the term *diffusion* or *innovation* or both terms in the title, but you wish to exclude the term *technology*. You are able to design a single search statement in this case, as each of the terms are found in the same field (i.e., the title). It is still, however, useful to conduct the search in stages to fully understand the implications of each step.

To begin your search, press the **ALT** key and **F** key simultaneously to obtain the field list, use the arrow key to highlight the field you wish to select (title), and tap the **ENTER** key.

You are now presented with the opportunity to type in the terms on which you wish to search:

Diffusion OR Innovation NOT Technology

While the above search statement establishes what you wish to retrieve, a more practical approach is to conduct the search in stages.

Step 1: Diffusion OR Innovation

This search will result in the following:

Records	Search Terms
25	Diffusion
112	Innovation

To obtain the results of your search, tap the **F4** key and select the Show Full Records option from the menu and tap the **ENTER** key.

No.	Records	Field
#1	134	Title DIFFUSION OR INNOVATION

As shown above, you will obtain a set containing 134 records. If you examine the above results, you can establish the way in which the terms combine. For example, while there are 25 records with the term *diffusion* in the title, and 112 records with the term *innovation* in the title, you retrieve 134 records. As you retrieve titles containing either the term *diffusion* or the term innovation or those titles that contain both terms, you obtain more than simply the sum of the two sets.

As it is your intention, however, to exclude those records that are concerned with technology, you will also need to use the **NOT** operator.

Step 2: SET 1(Diffusion OR Innovation) NOT Technology

To proceed with the above question, you will need to conduct a search for the term *technology* and establish a set. The illustration below is achieved when the term technology is sought:

No.	Records	Field
#1	134	Title DIFFUSION OR INNOVATION
#2	496	Title TECHNOLOGY

To finish the search you now need to combine the two sets using the **NOT** operator. To select the set field you need to tap the **ALT** key and the **F** key simultaneously. This action will retrieve the field selection menu. The Sets option is the last option on the menu; to select it, highlight the option and tap the **ENTER** key. At this point, you may type in **1 NOT 2**. This should achieve a result set that contains records with the terms *diffusion* or *innovation* and excludes the term *technology*, as shown below:

No.	Records	Field
#1	134	Title DIFFUSION OR INNOVATION
#2	496	Title TECHNOLOGY
#3	115	Set 1 NOT 2

To display the results of your search, tap the **F4** key and select the Show Full Records option from the menu and tap the **ENTER** key. You will obtain a set containing 115 records.

ADVANCED FEATURES

Limit Option

The limit option is activated by tapping the **ALT** key and the **L** key simultaneously. This action presents you with the following limit options:

Language: _____

Document type: _____

Update period: _____

To select the first option, Language, you need to tap the highlighted key, the **L** key. This will bring you to a list of the languages in which the documents have been written. To select a specific language you must highlight it and tap the **ENTER** key. The space to the right of the heading Language should now contain the selected language. The limit options of the Document type and Update work in a similar manner to the Language option.

Collect (Marking Records)

An important feature that is available at any point in the **F4**-Results section is the Collect feature. It is the Collect feature that allows you to mark records for later downloading, printing, or even making a set from the collected records. The Collect option is available in the lower menu while records are being viewed. The Collect option allows you to either collect (mark) the current record or the entire set of records. Using the Collect feature will also remove duplicate records. This is especially useful when collecting sets of Related Records[TM]. A searcher may quickly select several sets of records, knowing that only unique records will be collected. Once the records are "collected," they may be displayed using the

F4-Results option. This will allow you to view the collected records, print the collected records, or download the records to a file of your choice.

Save (Downloading)

The Save option allows you to download records as an ASCII text file. The file may be named by you but the file's extension will be set to .RPT. The downloading options allow you to select the current record for downloading or the entire set of records.

PRINTING AND DOWNLOADING DOCUMENTS

You are able to choose from the following print options:

This Record — this option allows you to print the record that is currently displayed.

Full Set — this option allows you to print all the records retrieved in the current search.

Collection — this option allows you to print what you previously collected (for printing or downloading).

The following options are available to determine the record format that will be printed:

Short record — the record's bibliographic details, the author, title, and journal details. The number or Related Records™ and references are given.

Record + address — the short record and the authors' addresses.

Record + references — the short record and the record's reference list.

Long record — the short record, the record's reference list, and the author's addresses.

Custom Record	– with this option you are able to designate as many or as few fields as you wish.

The records may be downloaded in one of the following file formats:

Plain text	– the records are saved in the form they appear on the screen.
DIALOG-ISI format	– the record's fields are tagged to conform with the DIALOG format.
Comma-delimited	– the record is saved in a format that may be imported directly into database programs.
Pro-Cite format	– the record is saved in a format that may be imported directly into Pro-Cite.
Tagged	– the record's fields are tagged with a two-letter code. The records may be imported directly into Sci-Mate.
NLM-Medline	– the record's fields are tagged to conform with the Medline format.

The following options are available to determine the record format that will be downloaded:

Short record	– the record's bibliographic details, the author, title, and journal details. The number or Related Records™ and references are given.
Record + address	– the short record and the authors' addresses.
Record + references	– the short record and the record's reference list.
Long record	– the short record, the record's reference list and the author's addresses.

Custom Record – with this option you are able to designate as many or as few fields as you wish.

SUMMARY

In this chapter you have been introduced to citation indexes. You should have an understanding of the following:

   a. Citation indexes are useful in that they allow you to retrieve documents that cite a particular work authored by a particular individual.
   b. The citation indexes allow you to find:
      – citations of a work
      – reviews of a work
      – locations of works that share common citations
      – documents searched by author or title
   c. Citation indexes are useful for discovering an author's institutional affiliation.
   d. The procedure for using the Boolean operators with ISI® indexes.
   e. The procedure for downloading and printing records.

Appendix A:
A Summary List of the Major CD ROMs by Subject Area

Product	Vendor	Type	Time Coverage	Update Frequency
AGRICULTURE				
Agricola	SilverPlatter	Bibliographic	1970-present	Quarterly
AGRIS	SilverPlatter	Bibliographic	1986-present	Quarterly
CAB Abstracts	SilverPlatter	Bibliographic	1984-present	Annually
ARCHITECTURE				
Architecture	AUSTROM	Bibliographic	1980-present	Quarterly
ART				
Art Index	H W Wilson	Bibliographic	1984-present	Quarterly
Art Room	Image Club Graphics	Graphic	1988 1st issue	Annual
BUSINESS AND FINANCE				
ABI/Inform	University Microfilms International	Bibliographic	1985-present	Quarterly

Product	Vendor	Type	Time Coverage	Update Frequency
BUSINESS AND FINANCE cont....				
Business Periodicals Index	H W Wilson	Bibliographic	1982-present	Quarterly
Business Periodicals Ondisc	University Microfilms International	Full Text	1987-present	Monthly
Canadian Business and Current Affairs	Dialog	Bibliographic	1981-present	Quarterly
Moody's 5000 Plus	Moody's Investor Service	Data/Statistics	1989-present	Quarterly
Moody's International Plus	Moody's Investor Service	Data/Statistics	1989-present	Quarterly
CHEMISTRY/ CHEMICAL				
Chem-Bank	SilverPlatter	Bibliographic	1988-present	Quarterly
Pest-Bank	SilverPlatter, Microinfo, Next	Bibliographic	1988-present	Quarterly
COMPUTER SCIENCE & ELECTRONICS				
Computer (tm)	Lotus Bluefish Ziff Communications Company	Full Text	1988-present	Monthly
INSPEC	University Microfilms International	Bibliographic	1989-present	Quarterly

Appendix A 183

Product	Vendor	Type	Time Coverage	Update Frequency

ECONOMICS

Product	Vendor	Type	Time Coverage	Update Frequency
EconLit	SilverPlatter	Bibliographic	1969-present	Quarterly

EDUCATION

Product	Vendor	Type	Time Coverage	Update Frequency
Australian Education Index (AEI)	AUSTROM	Bibliographic	1978-present	Quarterly
EDLINE	AUSTROM	Bibliographic	1980-present	Quarterly
Education Index	H W Wilson	Bibliographic	1983-present	Quarterly
Education Library/OCLC Asia/Pacific	OCLC	Catalogue	1987-present	Annually
ERIC	Dialog SilverPlatter	Bibliographic	1969-present	Quarterly
International Encyclopaedia of Education	Pergamon Compact Solution, Microinfo, Optech	Full Text	1988 1st issue	_____

ENVIRONMENT

Product	Vendor	Type	Time Coverage	Update Frequency
Aquatic Sciences and Fisheries Abstracts	Cambridge Scientific Abstracts	Bibliographic	1982-present	Quarterly
Chem-Bank with TOSCA	SilverPlatter, Microinfo	Textual/ Factual	1979-present	Quarterly
Earth Sciences- OCLC/Asia/ Pacific	OCLC	Bibliographic/ Graphic	1975-present	Quarterly
Environmental Periodicals	Environmental Studies Institutes	Bibliographic	1973-present	Semiannually

Product	Vendor	Type	Time Coverage	Update Frequency
ENVIRONMENT cont....				
Water Resources Abstracts	National Information Services Corporation	Bibliographic	1967-present	Semiannually
Biological & Agricultural Index	H.W. Wilson	Bibliographic	_____	Quarterly
GOVERNMENT				
GPO Monthly Catalog-US Government Publications & Periodicals	H W Wilson	Bibliographic	1976-present	Annually
Government Publications Index	IAC	Bibliographic	1976-present	Monthly
PAIS on CD-ROM	Public Affairs Information Service SilverPlatter	Bibliographic	1972-present	Quarterly
HUMANITIES				
Biography Index	H W Wilson	Bibliographic	1984-present	Quarterly
Essay and General Literature Index	H W Wilson	Bibliographic	1985-present	Annually
Humanities Index	H W Wilson	Bibliographic	1984-present	Quarterly
MLA International Bibliography	H W Wilson	Bibliographic	1981-present	Quarterly

Appendix A 185

Product	Vendor	Type	Time Coverage	Update Frequency
HUMANITIES cont. . . .				
Oxford English Dictionary	Oxford Electronic Publishing, Tri-star, Microinfo, Optech, Next, Attica	Dictionary/ Directory	1987 1st issue	
LEISURE				
Leisure	AUSTROM	Bibliographic	1982-present	Quarterly
Sport Discus	SilverPlatter	Bibliographic	1975-present	Semiannually
LIBRARY AND INFORMATION SCIENCE				
BiblioFile /LC Marc English	Library Corporation	Library Catalog (Database)	1985-present	Monthly
Directory of Library and Information Professionals	American Library Association	Bibliographic	1988-present	Biannually
Library Literature	H W Wilson	Bibliographic	1984-present	Quarterly
LISA	SilverPlatter, Attica	Bibliographic	1969-present	Semiannually
LITERATURE				
Disclit: American Authors/OCLC-Asia/Pacific	OCLC	Full Text/ Bibliographic		Annually

Product	Vendor	Type	Time Coverage	Update Frequency

LITERATURE cont . . . .

Product	Vendor	Type	Time Coverage	Update Frequency
Essay and General Literature Index	H W Wilson	Bibliographic	1985-present	Annually
Shakespeare on Disc	CMC Research Inc.	Full Text	_____	Annually

MATHEMATICS

Product	Vendor	Type	Time Coverage	Update Frequency
MathSci Disc Set	SilverPlatter	Bibliographic	1983-present	Semiannually

MEDICAL

Product	Vendor	Type	Time Coverage	Update Frequency
Cancer on Disc: 1989	SilverPlatter	Bibliographic Full Text (from 1988)	1984-present	Quarterly
Cancerlit	Cambridge Scientific Abstracts	Bibliographic	1985-present	Quarterly
CINAHL-CD	SilverPlatter	Bibliographic	1979-present	Microinfo
Medline	Cambridge Scientific Abstracts	Bibliographic	1966-present	Monthly
Medline	SilverPlatter	Bibliographic	1966-present	Monthly
Nursing and Allied Health (CINAHL)-CD	Cambridge Scientific Abstracts	Bibliographic	1983-present	Monthly
OSH-ROM	SilverPlatter	Bibliographic	1960-present	Quarterly

MULTI-DISCIPLINARY

Product	Vendor	Type	Time Coverage	Update Frequency
Books in Print Plus	R R Bowker Microinfo, Attica, Next	Bibliographic	1986-present	Bimonthly

Appendix A

Product	Vendor	Type	Time Coverage	Update Frequency

MULTI-DISCIPLINARY cont....

Product	Vendor	Type	Time Coverage	Update Frequency
Bookshelf/ Microsoft	Microsoft Corporation	Full Text	1987 1st issue	Irregular
Canadian Business and Current Affairs	Dialog Information Services, Inc.	Bibliographic	1981-present	Quarterly
Cumulative Book Index	H W Wilson, Attica	Bibliographic	1982-present	Quarterly
Drug Information Source on CD ROM	Cambridge Scientific Abstracts	Bibliographic/ Full Text	_____	Semiannual
General Periodicals Ondisc	University Microfilms International	Full Text	1989-present	Monthly
New Grolier Encyclopaedia	Grolier Electronic Pub. EBSCO, Optech, Next, Attica	Full Text	1986 1st issue	Irregular
Oxford English Dictionary	Oxford Electronic Pub. Tri-star, Next Microinfo, Optech, Attica	Dictionary/ Directory	1987 1st issue	_____
Readers' Guide Abstracts	H W Wilson	Bibliographic	1984-present	Quarterly
Readers' Guide to Periodical Literature	H W Wilson	Bibliographic	1983-present	Quarterly
Ulrich's Plus	R R Bowker, Microinfo, Next, Attica	Bibliographic	1986-present	Quarterly

Product	Vendor	Type	Time Coverage	Update Frequency

MUSIC

Product	Vendor	Type	Time Coverage	Update Frequency
Music Cataloguing Collection, OCLC-Asia/ Pacific	OCLC	Bibliographic	_____	Quarterly
Music Library OCLC/ Europe	OCLC	Bibliographic	_____	Annually

SCIENCE

Product	Vendor	Type	Time Coverage	Update Frequency
Appliede Scienc and Technology Index	H W Wilson	Bibliographic	1983-present	Quarterly
Biological/ RRM Abstracts on C D 1990	SilverPlatter	Bibliographic	1989-present	Quarterly
General Science Index	H W Wilson	Bibliographic	1984-present	Quarterly
INSPEC	University Microfilms International	Bibliographic	1989-present	Quarterly
McGraw-Hill Science and Technical Reference Set	McGraw-Hill Book Company, Microinfo, Attica	Full Text	1987 1st issue	Irregular
NTIS- National Technical Information	SilverPlatter, Microinfo, Next	Bibliographic	1983-present	Quarterly
Science Citation Index (SCI-CD)	Institute for Scientific Information	Bibliographic	1980-present	Quarterly
Science Helper K-8	PC SIG, Inc.	Bibliographic	1987 1st issue	Irregular

Product	Vendor	Type	Time Coverage	Update Frequency

SOCIAL SCIENCES

Product	Vendor	Type	Time Coverage	Update Frequency
Essay and General Literature Index	H W Wilson	Bibliographic	1985-present	Annually
PsycLit Social Sciences Citation Index	SilverPlatter Institute for Scientific Information	Bibliographic Citation Index	1974-present 1986-present	Quarterly Quarterly
Social Sciences Index	H W Wilson	Bibliographic Full Text	1983-present 1989-present	Quarterly Monthly
SocioFile	SilverPlatter, Microinfo	Bibliographic	1974-present	Triannually

TECHNOLOGY

Product	Vendor	Type	Time Coverage	Update Frequency
EI Energy and Environment	Dialog Information Services, Inc.	Bibliographic	1980-present	Quarterly
Energy library/ OCLC-Asia Pacific	OCLC	Bibliographic	_____	Annually
Food Science and Technology Abstracts (FSTA)	SilverPlatter	Bibliographic	1969-present	Annually
NTIS Database/ Dialog	Dialog Information Services, Inc.	Bibliographic	1980-present	Annually
NTIS Database	SilverPlatter	Bibliographic	1983-present	Quarterly

Appendix B: Glossary

Abstract –A brief precis or description of a book or journal article.

AND–One of the three Boolean operators. The **AND** operator requires *both* of the terms linked by it to be in the same record.

Bibliographic Database–A database of information in the form of records that identify works, documents, or bibliographic items.

Bibliography–An alphabetical list of works, documents, or bibliographic items with some shared relationships (e.g., referenced in a particular work).

Boolean logic–The principles that control the use of the Boolean operators **AND, OR,** and **NOT.**

Boolean operators–A set of three operators–the **AND, OR,** and **NOT** operators–that may be used to control ondisc searching.

Call number–A set of characters attached to an item to identify it in a library collection and to give it a specific shelf location.

Card Catalogue–A set of cards arranged in an alphabetical sequence that refer to items held in a library collection.

CD ROM–The acronym for Compact Disc Read Only Memory.

Character–A single letter, or the smallest element in a word.

Citation–The segment of a record that gives sufficient details to locate the document that the record represents.

Controlled vocabulary–A specific and exclusive list of subject terms that are selected to represent concepts. Access to the controlled vocabulary of a database is usually available via a thesaurus.

Database–An organized collection of related records.

Descriptor field–A field within a record that contains those subject terms which identify the subject content of the article that the record represents.

DOS–The acronym for Disc Operating System. It refers to the operating system used on IBM microcomputers or IBM-compatible microcomputers. DOS is also used to refer to IBM or IBM-compatible microcomputers (i.e., a DOS machine).

Downloading–The process that allows you to transfer or copy a retrieved record to your own floppy disc or hard drive.

Drive–The component of a microcomputer that records or stores information to a disc. A drive may take a floppy disc, or it may be a fixed or hard drive whose "disc" is part of the drive.

Field-specific searching–A type of search directed toward seeking information within the confines of a particular field.

Floppy disc–A portable storage device used in conjunction with a microcomputer drive. Typically a floppy disc will be either 3 1/2" or 5 1/4" in size.

Format–An ordered arrangement of a computer disc for storage that arranges locations for information into sections or sectors.

Full-text database–A database that contains the entire or full text of a publication or information service rather than a bibliographic representation. A typical example of a full-text database is a newspaper database in which the entire text of the newspaper is available.

Graphic database–A database that consists primarily of images or pictures rather than text.

IBM–The registered name for International Business Machine Corporation. It is commonly used to refer to a particular type of microcomputer.

Identifier field–A field within a record that contains subject terms or phrases which provide subject access to a record. Unlike the terms found in the descriptor field, the terms found in the identifier field are not considered to be controlled vocabulary and are therefore not found in a thesaurus.

Index–An alphabetical or ordered list of terms found within a database.

Keywords–Words or terms that refer to a subject concept or a particular person, place, or thing; typically a noun.

Limiting–A method of restricting or narrowing a search by use of Boolean logic, field-specific searching, or a combination of the two methods.

Logical operators–Boolean operators that allow you to broaden or restrict a search; the **AND, OR,** and **NOT** operators that may be used to control ondisc searching.

Macintosh–The registered name for a type of microcomputer.

Mark–The identification of a particular text element or record for later use, typically for downloading or printing.

Menu–A range of actions or options from which a selection may be made.

Microcomputer–A computer that typically has a single microprocessor; commonly referred to as a PC or Personal Computer.

Network–A communications system that links two or more computers.

NOT–The Boolean operator that excludes a specific term from a search.

Ondisc–Refers to the information stored on CD ROMs.

OPAC–The acronym for Online Public Access Catalog, typically used to refer to a particular library catalog.

OR–The Boolean operator that broadens a search so that it will include either of the linked terms.

Prefix–Used to refer to the characters or word element affixed to the beginning of a search term. It is typically used to limit a search to a particular field (e.g., **au(jones)** would limit the request for Jones to the author field).

Printer–A device or component of a computer system that produces printed output on paper.

Proximity operators–Terms, such as *with, near,* and *same,* used to associate two or more terms and establish a proximate relationship, typically within a number of words, a sentence, or a paragraph.

Records–The basic components of a database. A bibliographic record will typically consist of a citation, subject indexing terms, and an abstract.

Save–A command that allows you to "save" or download records retrieved from a search.

Searching–The process of seeking information from a database of records.

Shelf number–A number attached to an item to give it a specific location in a library collection.

Statistical database–A database of information that primarily consists of statistical data.

Stem–A term used to describe the "stem" or trunk portion of a term.

Suffix–Used to refer to the characters or word element affixed to the end of a term. It is typically used to limit a search to a particular file (e.g., **jones/au** would limit the request for Jones to the author field).

Thesaurus–A list of terms (synonyms and antonyms) that constitute the controlled or authorized vocabulary of a database. Terms found in the thesaurus will correspond with the terms found in the descriptor field of a record.

Trunk–See **Stem**.

Uploading–The retrieving of records that have been previously saved or downloaded to a disc. Typically the records are uploaded into a database or word processing program.

Venn diagrams–Circular drawings that are used to demonstrate the effect of Boolean operators.

SELECTED BIBLIOGRAPHY

Borgman, Christine. *Effective online searching: A basic text*. New York: M. Dekker, 1984.
Chen, Ching-chih, and Schweizer, Susanna. *Online bibliographic searching: A learning manual*. New York: Neal-Schuman Publishers, 1981.
Fenichel, Carol H. *Online searching: A primer*. 2nd ed. Marlton, NJ: Learned Information, 1984.
Hartley, R.J. *Online searching principles and practice*. London: Bowker, 1989.
Meadow, Charles T., and Cochran, Pauline Atherton. *Basics of online searching*. New York: Wiley, 1981.
Tenopir, Carol. *Issues in online database searching*. Englewood, CO: Libraries Unlimited, 1989.

Index

Page numbers in italics indicate figures.

AB (Abstract field), 32
ABI/INFORM Ondisc (UMI)
    downloading, 108-110
    field-specific searching, 32-34
    initial menu, 98-104
    range of information, 6-7,95-96
    subject searching, 105-108
Abstract, defined, 7,191
Abstract field (AB), 32
    Australian Public Affairs
        Information Service (APAIS),
        136
Agriculture databases, 181
ALT key in rebooting, 42,44
American spelling, 25,68
AND operator
    defined, 191
    DIALOG, 51,55-56
    Health database (Compact
        Cambridge), 114-115
    ISI Citation Indexes, 173-174
    LEISURE, 137-138,140-144
    New Grolier Electronic
        Encyclopedia, 158-159
    SilverPlatter-PsycLIT, 68-71,72
    use of, 16,*17*,26
APAIS. *See* Australian Public
    Affairs Information Service
Applied Science & Technology
    (WILSONDISC), 82
ARCH (Australian Architecture
    Database), 132
Architecture databases, 132,181
Art databases, 81,181
Art Index (WILSONDISC), 81

AU (Author field). *See* Author field
    (AU)
AUSPORT, 132
Australian Architecture Database
    (ARCH), 132
Australian Architecture Database
    (ARCH), 132
Australian Criminology Database
    (CINCH), 132
    Boolean searching, 148-150
Australian Education Index (AEI),
    131-132
Australian Family and Society
    Abstracts (FAMILY), 133
Australian Index to Leisure
    Activities and Consumer
    Reports (PINPointer), 133
Australian Public Affairs
    Information Service (APAIS),
    132
    Boolean searching, 148-150
    downloading, 150-151
    field-specific searching, 136-140
    printing, 151
    record structure, 133-136
Australian Schools Catalogue
    Information Service
    (Curriculum Resources
    Abstracts) (ASCIS-CRA),
    132
AUSTROM searching, 131-151
    Boolean searching
        AND, 140-144
        NOT, 148-150
        OR, 144-147

197

downloading, 150-151
field-specific searching, 136-140
printing, 151
record structure, 133-136
sources of information, 6,131-133
Author field (AU), 32
   Australian Public Affairs
      Information Service (APAIS),
      134-135
   in field-specific searches, 34-36
   ISI Citation Indexes,
      168-169,173-174

B (Broader Term), 22-23, 65-66
Bibliographic record, fields,
   29-30,36-37
Bibliography, defined, 191
Biography Index (WILSONDISC),
   82
Boolean searching
   Australian Criminology Database
      (CINCH), 148-150
   Australian Public Affairs
      Information Service (APAIS),
      137-138,144-147
   defined, 191
   DIALOG, 51,55-59
   elements, 5-6
   in field-specific searches, 35
   Health database (Compact
      Cambridge), 114-117
   ISI Citation Indexes, 173-176
   LEISURE, 140-144
   New Grolier Electronic
      Encyclopedia, 158-159
   SilverPlatter-PsycLIT
      AND, 68-71
      NOT, 72-78
      OR, 67-68
   using operators, 16-20,*17,18,*
      *19,*26
   WILSONDISC, 90
Bowling Green State University, 49
Brackets, 20-21, *21,*26

British spelling, 68
Broader Terms (B), 22-23,65-66
Business databases, 181-182
   ABI/INFORM (UMI)
      fields, 32-34
      range of information, 6-7,95-96
      searching, 98-104
   Business Dateline Ondisc (UMI), 96
   Business Periodicals Index
      (WILSONDISC), 82

Call number, defined, 191
Card catalogue
   defined, 191
   locating material, 10
CD ROM (Compact Disc Read Only
   Memory). *See also* Ondisc
   searching
   advantages, 1
   disc, 8
   reader, 8
Character, defined, 191
Check Disk (CHKDSK) command,
   41
Chemistry/chemical databases, 182
CINCH. *See* Australian Criminology
   Database
CINCH (Australian Criminology
   Database), 132, 148-150
Citations, defined, 7,191
CO (Company field) in
   ABI/INFORM, 32
Combining terms
   Australian Criminology Database
      (CINCH), 149
   Australian Public Affairs
      Information Service (APAIS),
      137-138,146
   explanation of technique, 23-24
   LEISURE, 140-142
Compact Cambridge searching,
   111-129
   command searching, 120-124
   downloading, 129
   fields, 112-113

Index

field-specific searching, 124-129
initial menu, 113
menu searching, 113-119
sources of information, 111-112
Company field (CO) in ABI/
INFORM, 32
Computers. *See* Microcomputers
Computer science databases, 182
Controlled vocabulary, defined, 192
Controlled Vocabulary Searching
DIALOG, 57
explanation of technique, 22-23
Criminology databases, 132,148-150
CTRL key in rebooting, 42,44
Cumulative Book Index
(WILSONDISC), 82-83

Databases. *See also specific products*
AUSTROM, 131-151
categories, 7-8
Compact Cambridge, 111-129
defined, 192
DIALOG, 47-62
information available, 6-7
ISI®Citation Indexes, 165-180
New Grolier Electronic
Encyclopedia, 153-164
SilverPlatter, 63-80
UMI, 95-109
WILSONDISC, 81-93
DEL key in rebooting, 42,44
Descriptor field, 7,30,32
Australian Public Affairs
Information Service (APAIS),
135,137-138
defined, 192
DIALOG, 57
SilverPlatter PsycLIT, 65-66,68
DIALOG ondisc searching, 47-62
Command Search mode, 52-59
Boolean searching, 55-59
downloading and printing,
61-62

Easy Menu Search mode
Boolean searching, 51
downloading and printing, 52
sources of information, 47-48
Philosopher's Index, 49
truncation, 59-60
Dictionary in ISI®Citation Indexes,
169-173
Disc drives
defined, 192
types of, 39-40
Dissertation Abstracts ondisc (UMI),
97
field-specific searching, 104-105
subject searching, 105-108
DOS, defined, 192
DOS commands, 41
Double-density drives, 39-40
Downloading, 8
Australian Public Affairs
Information Service (APAIS),
150-151
defined, 192
DIALOG, 52,61-62
Health database (Compact
Cambridge), 129
ISI®Citation Indexes, 178-180
New Grolier Electronic
Encyclopedia, 162-163
procedure, 42-43
SilverPlatter-PsycLIT database,
79-80
UMI database, 108-109
WILSONDISC, 92-93
Drives
defined, 192
types of, 39-40

Economics databases, 183
EDLINE, 132-133
Education databases, 183
Australian Education Index (AEI),
131-132

Australian Schools Catalogue
    Information Service
    (ASCIS-CRA), 132
AUSTROM, 6
EDLINE, 132-133
Education Index (WILSONDISC),
    83
Electronics databases, 182
Environment databases, 183-184

FAMILY (Australian Family and
    Society Abstracts), 133
Fields
  ABI/INFORM (UMI),
      32-34,98,102-104
  Australian Criminology Database
      (CINCH), 150
  Australian Public Affairs
      Information Service (APAIS),
      134-136
  in bibliographic record, 29-30,*30*
  DIALOG database, 49-51
  Dissertation Abstracts ondisc,
      104-105,106-108
  Health database (Compact
      Cambridge),
      112-113,117-119,122-124,
      126-129
  ISI®Citation Indexes, 167-169
  keys, 32-36
  LEISURE, 142-144
  New Grolier Electronic
      Encyclopedia, 159
  SilverPlatter PsycLIT, 64-65,
      69-71,73-78
  unsearchable, 31-32
  WILSONDISC, 86-89,92
Field-specific searching
  ABI/INFORM (UMI) Ondisc,
      104-105
  advantages, 31
  Australian Public Affairs
      Information Service (APAIS),
      136-140

database-specificity of, 31-32
DIALOG, 52-55
example of, 32-36
explanation of, 25-26,27,192
SilverPlatter-PsycLIT, 68,78
typical abbreviations, 32
WILSONDISC, 91-92
File extension, 42
File name, 42
Find prompt in SilverPlatter-PsycLIT
    database, 66-67
Floppy disc, defined, 192
Floppy disc drive, 39-40
Format, defined, 192
Formatting discs, 40-41
Free text searching in PsycLIT
    database, 66
Full-text database, defined, 192
Function keys, 41

General Science Index
    (WILSONDISC), 83
Government databases, 184
Graphic database
  defined, 192
  New Grolier Electronic
      Encyclopedia, 155
Grolier Encyclopedia. *See* New
    Grolier Electronic
    Encyclopedia

Health database (Compact
    Cambridge), 112-113
HEI (Home Economics Index), 133
High-density drives, 39-40
Home Economics Index (HEI), 133
Humanities databases, 184-185
Humanities Index (WILSONDISC),
    83-84

IBM computers, 39
Identifier field (ID), 7,30,32
  Australian Public Affairs
      Information Service (APAIS),
      135,136

defined, 193
LEISURE, 144
ID (Identifier field). *See* Identifier field (ID)
Index, defined, 193
Index to Legal Periodicals (WILSONDISC), 84
Information sciences databases, 185
INSPEC ondisc (UMI), 98
ISI®Citation Indexes, 165-180
   Boolean searching, 173-176
   dictionary, 169-173
   limit option, 177
   marking records, 177-178
   printing and downloading, 178-180
   record structure, 168-169
   searching procedures, 166-168
   sources of information, 165-166

Keyboard components, 41-42
Key concepts
   combining, 15-16
   identifying, 14-15
Keywords
   combining, 15-16
   defined, 193
   identifying, 14-15

Lateral searching in SilverPlatter-PsycLIT database, 78
Legal periodical databases, 84
LEISURE database, 133
   Boolean searching, 140-147
Leisure databases. *See* Sports databases
Library Literature Index (WILSONDISC), 84
Library science databases, 185
Limiting, defined, 193
Limit Options field in DIALOG database, 50
Literature databases, 185-186

Logical operators. *See* Boolean searching

Macintosh computers, 43-44
Major descriptors (MJ). *See* Descriptor field
Marking records, 42
   defined, 193
   ISI®Citation Indexes, 177-178
   SilverPlatter PsycLIT, 78-79
   UMI database, 108-109
Mathematics databases, 186
Medical databases, 186
Melbourne, Australia, 133
Menu, defined, 193
Microcomputers, 39-44
   CD ROM workstation, 8,9
   defined, 193
   downloading, 42-43
   formatting discs, 40-41
   keyboard, 41-42
   Macintosh, 43-44
   types of, 39-40
   uploading or printing, 43
Minor Descriptors (MN). *See* Descriptor field
MJ (Major Descriptors). *See* Desriptor field
MN (Minor Descriptors). *See* Descriptor field
Multi-disciplinary databases, 186-187
Music databases, 188

Narrower terms (N), 22-23,65-66
National Library of Medicine (USA), 112
Network, defined, 193
New Grolier Electronic Encyclopedia, 153-164
   advanced searching techniques, 155-162
   BookMarks, 163-164
   full-text searching, 153-155

Link, 164
NotePad, 162-163
picture retrieval, 155
pull-down menus, 162
Newspaper Abstracts ondisc (UMI), 96-97
N (Narrower terms), 22-23, 65-66
NOT operator, 18, *18*, 26
   Australian Criminology Database (CINCH), 148-150
   defined, 193
   in DIALOG, 51, 55-56
   Health database (Compact Cambridge), 114-115
   ISI Citation Indexes, 174-176
   New Grolier Electronic Encyclopedia, 158-159
   SilverPlatter PsycLIT, 72-78

Ondisc, defined, 194
Ondisc searching. *See also specific databases*
   AUSTROM, 131-151
      downloading, 150-151
      printing, 151
      searching procedures, 133-150
      sources of information, 131-133
   basic components, 7
   basic steps
      combining keywords, 15-16
      creating search question, 13-14
      identifying keywords, 14-15
   Compact Cambridge, 111-129
      downloading, 129
      searching, 112-129
      sources of information, 111-112
   databases, 7-8
   defined, 5-6
   DIALOG, 47-62
      downloading and printing, 61-62
      sources of information, 47-59
      truncation, 59-60
      equipment, 8, 9, 10
   information available, 6-7
   ISI®Citation Indexes, 165-180
      Boolean searching, 173-176
      dictionaries, 169-173
      printing and downloading, 178-180
      record structure, 168-169
      searching, 166-168, 177-178
      sources of information, 165-166
   locating the material, 8-10
   New Grolier Electronic Encyclopedia, 153-164
   SilverPlatter, 63-80
      downloading, 79-80
      printing, 79
      record structure, 64-65
      searching procedures, 66-79
      sources of information, 63-64
      thesaurus, 65-66
   techniques, 26, 28
      Boolean logic, 16-20, *17, 18, 19*
      brackets, 20-21
      combining terms, 23-24
      controlled vocabulary, 22-23
      field-specific searching, 25-26, 31
      proximity operators, 24
      spelling, 25
      stopwords, 24-25
      truncation, 23
   UMI, 95-109
      downloading, 108-109
      searching procedures, 98-108
      sources of information, 95-98
   WILSONDISC, 81-93
      downloading and printing, 92-93
      searching procedures, 85-92
      sources of information, 81-84
Ondisc thesaurus, SilverPlatter-PsycLIT database, 66
Online Public Access Catalogue (OPAC), 10, 194
Online searching vs. ondisc searching, 5

OPAC (Online Public Access
     Catalogue)
  defined, 194
  locating material, 10
OR operator, 16-18, *17*,26
  Australian Public Affairs
     Information Service (APAIS),
     144-147
  defined, 194
  DIALOG, 51,55-56,60
  Health database (Compact
     Cambridge), 115-116
  ISI®Citation Indexes, 175
  New Grolier Electronic
     Encyclopedia, 158-159
  SilverPlatter PsycLIT, 67-68,72
  and spelling variations, 25

Periodical Abstracts ondisc (UMI),
     97
Personal Computers. *See*
     Microcomputers
Philosopher's Index database, 48
  Command Search mode, 52-59
  downloading and printing, 61-62
  Easy Menu Search mode, 49-52
  truncation, 59-60
Picture retrieval, 155
PINPointer (Australian Index to
     Leisure Activities and
     Consumer Reports), 133
Population field, 31
Prefix, defined, 194
Printer, defined, 194
Printing
  Australian Public Affairs
     Information Service (APAIS),
     151
  DIALOG, 52,61-62
  vs. downloading, 40
  ISI®Citation Indexes, 178-180
  New Grolier Electronic
     Encyclopedia, 162-163
  procedure, 43

SilverPlatter-PsycLIT, 79
WILSONDISC, 92-93
Proximity operators
  defined, 194
  explanation of, 24,27
PsycLIT database, 64-80
  Boolean searching
     AND, 68-71
     NOT, 72-78
     OR, 67-68
  downloading, 79-80
  fields, 31
  field-specific searching, 78
  Find prompt, 66-67
  lateral searching, 78
  marking records, 78-79
  printing, 79
  record structure, 64-65
  thesaurus, 65-66
Publication Year field (PY), 31,32
  SilverPlatter-PsycLIT database, 78
Pull-down menus, 162
PY (Publication Year field). *See*
     Publication Year field

Reader's Guide to Periodical
     Literature (WILSONDISC),
     84
Rebooting, 42
Records
  defined, 7,194
  marking, 42
     defined, 193
     ISI®Citation Indexes, 177-178
     SilverPlatter PsycLIT, 78-79
     UMI database, 108-109
Record structure
  ABI/INFORM (UMI) Ondisc,
     32-34,98,102-104
  Australian Criminology Database
     (CINCH), 150
  Australian Public Affairs
     Information Service (APAIS),
     134-136,138-139,146-147
  bibliographic records, 29-30

database-specificity of, 31-32
DIALOG, 49-51
Dissertation Abstracts ondisc
  (UMI), 104-105,106-108
fields
  explanation, 30
  keys, 32-36
Health database (Compact
  Cambridge), 112-113,117-
  119,122-124,126-129
ISI®Citation Indexes, 167-169,
  168-169
LEISURE, 142-144
New Grolier Electronic
  Encyclopedia, 159
sample of, 29-30
SilverPlatter PsycLIT, 64-65,
  69-71,73-78
WILSONDISC, 86-89
Related Terms (R), 22-23,65-66
Resource/One ondisc (UMI), 97
R (Related terms), 22-23,65-66

Save. *See* Downloading
Science databases, 181,182,183-184,
  188
  Applied Science & Technology
    (WILSONDISC), 82
  General Science Index
    (WILSONDISC), 83
  ISI Science Citation Index, 165
Scope Note (SN), 22,65-66
Searching, defined, 194. *See also*
  Databases: *specific products*
Search questions, creating, 13-14
Shelf number, defined, 194
SilverPlatter ondisc searching, 63-80
  Boolean searching
    AND, 68-71
    NOT, 72-78
    OR, 67-68
  downloading, 79-80
  field-specific searching, 78
  Find prompt, 66-67

lateral searching, 78
marking records, 78-79
printing, 79
PsycLIT, 64
record structure, 64-65
sources of information, 63-64
thesaurus, 65-66
SN (Scope Note), 22,65-66
Social sciences databases, 84,189
  AUSTROM, 6
  ISI®Social Sciences Citation
    Index, 165
Social Sciences Index
  (WILSONDISC), 84
SocioFile database, 75-78
Software. *See specific products*
Source field (SO), 30,32
Spelling variations, OR search,
  25,68
Sports databases, 185
  AUSPORT, 132
  Australian Index to Leisure
    Activities and Consumer
    Reports (PINPointer), 133
  LEISURE, 133,140-150
Statistical database, defined, 194
Stem, 59-60
  defined, 194
Stopwords, examples of, 24-25
Subject searching
  Dissertation Abstracts (UMI),
    105-108
  SilverPlatter PsycLIT, 65-66
Suffix, defined, 195

Technology databases, 189
Term field (TE), 32
Thesaurus
  Australian Public Affairs
    Information Service (APAIS),
    135
  and controlled vocabulary, 22
  defined, 195
  DIALOG, 57
  SilverPlatter-PsycLIT, 65-66

TI (Title field). *See* Title field
Title field (TI), 32
   Australian Public Affairs
      Information Service (APAIS),
      134
   ISI®Citation Indexes,
      169-170,174-176
Title searches, 154
Truncation operators
   DIALOG database, 59-61
   explanation of, 23,27
   in field-specific search, 36
   Health database (Compact
      Cambridge), 115-116
   SilverPlatter PsycLIT, 67
Trunk, 59-60,195

UMI ondisc searching, 95-109
   downloading, 108-109
   field-specific searching, 104-105
   initial menu, 98-104
   sources of information
      ABI/INFORM, 95-96
      Business Dateline Ondisc, 96
      Dissertation Abstracts ondisc, 97
      INSPEC ondisc, 98
      Newspaper Abstracts ondisc, 96-97
      Periodical Abstracts ondisc, 97
      Resource/One ondisc, 97
   subject searching, 105-108

University Microfilms International.
   See UMI ondisc searching
Uploading, defined, 195. *See also*
   Printing

Venn diagrams, defined, 195

WESTDOC, 133
WILSONDISC searching, 81-93
   downloading and printing, 92-93
   search modes
      BROWSE, 85-88
      WILSEARCH, 88-90
      WILSONLINE, 90-92
   sources of information
      Applied Science & Technology, 82
      Art Index, 81
      Biography Index, 82
      Business Periodicals Index, 82
      Cumulative Book Index, 82-83
      Education Index, 83
      General Science Index, 83
      Humanities Index, 83-84
      Index to Legal Periodicals, 84
      Library Literature Index, 84
      Reader's Guide to Periodical Literature, 84
      Social Sciences Index, 84
Wordperfect, 43
Word processing in uploading, 43
Workstation equipment, 8,9